REal Life EMPOWERED

BO PORTER

SECOND EDITION

Printed in the United States of America

Published by SuburbanBuzz.com, LLC

ISBN: 0-9896377-4-3
ISBN-13: 978-0-9896377-4-9

DEDICATION

"I can do all things through him who strengthens me."

~ Philippians 4:13 ESV

This book is dedicated to my Heavenly Father God for His unconditional everlasting love. We all have a Godly ordained opportunity to impact the space we reside in. God has long been there for me even before I ever knew Him. When I look at my life and the many obstacles I've faced, I now know no human being could have navigated this ship through its troubled waters. Now that I've grown in my Christian walk, I too want others to experience what it truly means to be a champion for Christ.

When we learn to humble ourselves, and submit to God, his plan for our lives become crystal clear! We hear him differently, see him differently, feel him differently and become EMPOWERED! You too can learn how to "let go"—and "grow"—with God!

It was Christmas Day 2011 and I received a life altering gift in the form of a book titled UNCOMMON LIFE By Tony Dungy and Nathan Whitaker. The impact of that book not only encouraged me to grow closer to God but it also inspired me to start my own Book Club. The spiritual messages were shared daily by text message. It started with twenty members on January 1, 2012 and quickly grow to an unknown number of spiritually feed members. Tony and Nathan thanks for being disciples of God and true servants of God's word.

The Book Club text message and email is a daily devotional and fellowship for its members. The spiritual food is sent daily to family, friends, prayer groups, colleagues, former teammates, classmates, professional athletes, coaches and corporate business leaders. The messages are then recirculated by others to their networks. So the actual number of God's children being feed by the daily messages is truly unknown. Witnessing the impact the Book Club was having in my life and others inspired me to expand my God given territory with the publishing of REal Life EMPOWERED. I pray the daily reading of this book helps you get plugged in and be a champion for Christ.

I am COMMITTED to being a Champion for Christ because God loved us so much He gave us His only son. I HUMBLY accept all the goodness my Father has bestowed upon me. Being AUTHENTIC has allowed me to live with complete faith and freedom. My core values are MORALLY enriched by my decision to follow the life of Christ. I wholeheartedly accepted my

PURPOSE to spread the word of God when I was baptized and accepted Jesus Christ as my Lord and Savior. Following Christ is an INTENTIONAL act to glorify God's Kingdom. Being OPPOSED to the world is a fight all Christians must battle every day. Repentance and transformational change are our only options to win that battle. My blessings are God's favor and His love is unconditional and NEVER-ENDING!

God, I thank you for your unwavering love even when I didn't deserve it. Your grace, mercy and favor has given me an abundance of spiritual strength. God I pray You continue to bless me and allow me the opportunity to glorify You.

TABLE OF CONTENTS

ACKNOWLEDGMENTS

God: First and foremost I want to thank my Heavenly Father for sending His only son to be my Lord and Savior. In my life's journey, God has met me wherever I was Spiritually and sent the right people into my life every step of the way. I am so thankful for your Mercy and Grace. May Your will be done.

Bryce: My amazing son, and the joy of my life. Bryce, thank you for being understanding when Daddy had to spend countless hours researching, writing and editing this book. It touched my heart when you included me in your daily prayer asking God, "God please let my daddy finish his book, so we can get back to having fun!" Bryce, God answered your prayer and we are back to having fun! Daddy loves you, Bryce!

Beverly Porter: My loving mother and the strongest woman I know. Witnessing you overcome the many obstacles and circumstances in your life truly helped shape and mold my mental toughness, work ethic and fortitude. My favorite Mother quote is, "I worked too hard for you not to end up successful." I can remember you telling me at an early age that God will always protect us. Mother, thank you for introducing me to the love of God.

Holly Chervnsik: Founder and Owner of SuburbanBuzz Publishing who first suggested *REal Life EMPOWERED* be my first published book. Holly, your experience, knowledge and collaboration helped me turn three years of book club messages and my personal walk with Christ and desire to share God's Word into this REal Life spiritual masterpiece. Thank you for your time, effort and patience throughout this entire project. Your finishing touches to the book were absolutely profound.

Shaye Henderson: Chief Editor and Data Researcher: Shaye, thank you for your tireless efforts, data research and editorial expertise. Your attention to detail and literacy guidance throughout this project kept me on track. Shaye, your commitment to excellence can be found in the completion of *REal Life EMPOWERED*. I was truly blessed to have you as the chief editor for this book. I'm thankful and grateful for all you put into making this project come to life. The next Starbucks is on me!

Minister Irving Johnson: My earthly father and whose life story is the best living example known to me, of God meeting one of His children where they are and bringing them home. My dad's spiritual journey has been an inspiration for me to live my life for Christ. My dad always ends our conversations by saying these three things: "Keep Christ first in your life, and you will always have a life," "Kiss your wife and hug your son," and "Daddy loves you!"

Baseball Chapel: My church away from home. Being blessed with an opportunity to have a career in sports means I travel a great portion of the year. With travel, come a lot of Sundays and Wednesdays without attending my traditional church service. Baseball Chapel has been the Spiritual food for many professional baseball players over the years. I want to thank all of our Chapel leaders, but I want to especially thank Tim Pierson, our Chapel leader in Washington DC, when I coached for the Washington Nationals. Tim's commitment to sharing God's Word and the personal interest he took in connecting and engaging in my Spiritual development was transformative.

David Yasko: My Minister at Westbury Church of Christ and one of my most faithful prayer warriors. David, your support, wisdom and prayers have always been uplifting. You are more than my Minister, you are my brother and a dear friend.

Bill Yasko: My retired Minister from Westbury Church of Christ and the man who witnessed my greatest earthly accomplishment. Bill was the Minister responsible for bringing me to Christ in baptism on February 28, 1999. Thank you Bill for your spiritual guidance.

Steve Foster: My brother in Christ. Your Spiritual inspiration and intellectual stimulation have not only strengthened my personal values but have also inspired my professional leadership principles as well. Witnessing your walk with Christ, breaking bread and sharing God's Word with you, helped me grow in Christ. That growth is evident throughout the words in this book. Thank you, brother, for being a part of my Spiritual journey.

Jim Goodrich: Campus Director of Athletes in Action at the University of Iowa. Jim, thank you for shaping the lives of young people at such an impressionable age. Your Spiritual guidance helped me build a strong foundation and has never been forgotten.

INTRODUCTION

GOD'S PLAN

How did the publishing of *REal Life EMPOWERED* occur? It happened in the blink of an eye, but it has actually been in the process stage for many years. I was sitting in a publishing meeting discussing the release details of my first book, *The End Game*. Suddenly a series of questions from the publisher surrounding the Spiritual Book Club I started three years ago derailed, or should I say REdirected, our conversation and inadvertently changed my author's path to its rightful starting point.

REal Life EMPOWERED was not scheduled to be my first published book. I thought my first book would be sports related, given the fact I have over twenty-two years of experience in professional sports, and I had been working extensively on *The End Game* for over a year.

So how did I get off track? Or am I right on track? Because I'm a believer, I know that my steps are already ordered. I followed the steering of my heart and stepped out on faith. After two months of reading, researching and reflecting how I arrived at this point, I'm convinced it was God's plan to publish *REal Life EMPOWERED* first! He placed me at the right place, at the right time and with the right people! Know this: when God has a plan for our life, nothing...I mean nothing, will be able to stop His plan. This project has allowed me to grow closer to God's Kingdom and has deepened my faith. It has given me more clarity about my relationship with God and my relationship with others, as well. I now have a better understanding of my responsibility to serve and be a vessel for God's countless messages to the world. The publishing of *REal Life EMPOWERED* was inspired by God and will bring its readers into God's Kingdom. So I am right on track. Thank you God for REdirecting my author's path!

PURPOSE OF THIS BOOK

I pray the reading of *REal Life EMPOWERED* daily devotional will educate your mind, enrich your heart and empower your soul. This enlightening one-year devotional will be your guide, every day, as you travel the path of REal Excellence. Having a daily appointment with God is a vital component of mastering our journey with Christ.

REal Excellence is a Godly process that you can access and build on each day to bring inspiration, abundance, and an ingrained prosperity into every aspect of your life.

Your transformation will begin the day you commit to reading this book daily with an open heart. Each devotional includes Scripture, a related quote and a "REism"—an application, action, thought-provoking statement or question that will resonate within your mind, body and soul.

The goal is to not only engage your mind, but also to penetrate your heart and draw you closer to God's Kingdom.

The book focuses on nine core values needed for whole-person development. These nine core values will provide its readers an EMPOWERED confidence of "The GOOD Life" promised to God's children.

Education

Manners

Physical Activity

Open-mindedness

Well-balanced Nutrition

Expression of Positive Attitude

Relationships

Enrichment of Spirit

Dedication

I pray you are committed to reading and applying God's Kingdom to your daily life. If for one reason or another you miss a day, it is important to continue moving forward. Don't be discouraged and don't feel the need to play catch up. Because this is a yearly devotional, a reader can start at any point within the book and consume the spiritual feeding provided daily. Remember our God is willing to meet you wherever you are. Jesus told the story of the prodigal son to make a simple point: never mind what you've done, just come home. So press forward and keep Christ first in your life, and you will always have a REwarding life.

REal Life EMPOWERED daily devotional will give its readers a defined direction and will be your bridge to a true authentic relationship with God. I pray this book not only cultivates change in your life, but also inspires you to share your newfound blessing with others in and out of your network and increases your spear of influence for God's glory.

THE POWER OF QUIET TIME WITH GOD

It was May 2013 when I received a text message from my mother, Beverly Porter. I opened the text and started reading the message, only to be interrupted by an incoming call from a former teammate.

Let me go on record now and state a very IMPORTANT fact about this message. To truly receive the greatest impact, please read it in its entirety, in a quiet place, with an open heart and mind.

I stopped and took the call from my friend. He was in need of help! Life had come tumbling down on him, and he was at a loss for answers. After an hour-long conversation, I sat quietly recapping our discussion. My heart felt his pain, and I was thinking of ways I could help. For the moment I had forgotten about the message my mother had sent. Yes, that extremely powerful message I started reading, but stopped when I received the incoming call from my friend.

Now in a quiet place I began praying for my friend. After praying for my friend I reopened the message from my mother and read it from beginning to end, not once, not twice, but I read it three times without interruption. The message was that good! So good in fact that I immediately forwarded it to my friend and asked him to find a quiet place to read the message. Quiet time with God in prayer and feeding our soul spiritual food is vital to our relationship with Christ. The next day I sent the message to our entire Book Club Family and encouraged them to read the message in a quiet place, as well. Be sure you are carving out your quiet time with God daily.

So what was the message?

GOD'S IMPORTANT REcall FOR ALL LIVING HUMAN BEINGS

The original author of GOD'S IMPORTANT REcall is Unknown. Where this message originated or how many different versions exist I don't know. But my research of GOD'S IMPORTANT REcall message led to the message being sent to John McTernan from one of his bloggers. I want to personally thank and acknowledge the blogger for a great post. John, thank you for sharing this impactful message. Last, but surely not least, I want to praise God and give Him the glory for placing this message into the heart and soul of one of His children.

This message has become a part of my journey with Christ and I pray it becomes a part of your journey with Christ as well. It is a great message to read, reflect upon and remind us of our relationship with Christ. We can also use this message if or when we ever need to be REdirected in our walk with Christ. Thanks for the text, Mother. I love you!

The Message: God's REcall Notice

You may have never heard it put quite like this before....but this message is totally amazing. Talk about clever and to the point! This message speaks in a modern day language that is RElatable, REtainable and REliable. One final request before you start reading the message: FIND A QUIET PLACE! I repeat, for greatest impact, please read in its entirety, in a quiet place, with an open heart and mind.

GOD'S REcall NOTICE:

The Maker of all human beings (GOD) is REcalling all units manufactured, regardless of make or year, due to a serious defect in the primary and central component of the heart.

This is due to a malfunction in the original prototype units, codenamed Adam and Eve, resulting in the reproduction of the same defect in all subsequent units.

This defect has been identified as "Subsequential Internal Non-morality," more commonly known as S.I.N., as it is primarily expressed.

Some of the symptoms include:

      1. Loss of direction

      2. Foul vocal emissions

      3. Amnesia of origin

      4. Lack of peace and joy

      5. Selfish or violent behavior

      6. Depression or confusion

      7. Fearfulness

      8. Idolatry

      9. Rebellion

The Manufacturer (GOD) who is neither liable nor at fault for this defect, is providing factory-authorized repair and service free of charge to correct this defect.

The Repair Technician, JESUS, has most generously offered to bear the entire burden of the staggering cost of these repairs. There is NO ADDITIONAL FEE required.

The number to call for repair in all areas is: P-R-A-Y-E-R. Once connected, please upload your burden of SIN through the REPENTANCE procedure.

Next, download ATONEMENT from the Repair Technician, Jesus, into the heart component.

No matter how big or small the SIN defect is, Jesus will replace it with:

- **E**ducation and knowledge of His Word

- **M**anners so we reflect kindness and forgiveness

- **P**hysical Activity because your body is your temple

- **O**pen-mindedness so we always have room for growth

- **W**ell-balanced Nutrition to feed the mind, body and soul

- **E**xpression of Positive Attitude because negative thoughts are draining

- **R**elationships to help surround you with other believers

- **E**nrichment of Spirit so we can be His light through all the darkness

- **D**edication that will yield external life to its followers and believers

Please see the Operating Manual, the B.I.B.L.E. for further details on the use of these fixes.

BIBLE Acronym:

- **B**est

- **I**nstructions

- **B**efore

- **L**eaving

- **E**arth

WARNING: Continuing to operate the human being unit without correction voids any manufacturer warranties, exposing the unit to dangers and problems too numerous to list, and will result in the human unit being permanently impounded. For free emergency service, call on Jesus.

DANGER: The human being units not responding to this REcall action will have to be scrapped in the furnace. The SIN defect will not be permitted to enter Heaven so as to prevent contamination of that facility. Thank you for your attention! --GOD

P.S. Please assist where possible by notifying others of this important REcall notice, because He has EMPOWERED you! Feel free to contact the Father any time by "knee mail"!

Working for God on Earth doesn't pay much in dollar value.....but His retirement plan is out of this world!

Have you taken your unit to the manufacturer, God?

If not, please do so before your time expires.

After reading this IMPORTANT REcall MESSAGE, you now realize the seriousness of this REcall. Drop everything and get in to see GOD, NOW! It's not too late. He is open 24 hours a day, 7 days a week and 365 days a year.

After reading this message, I hope you are committed to keeping your daily appointment with God. During the coming year, *REal Life EMPOWERED* daily devotional can help by giving you 365 days of spiritual guidance. *REal Life EMPOWERED* provides a daily opportunity to connect with God's Kingdom and experience the power of His Word.

Enjoy *REal Life EMPOWERED* daily devotional and Happy New Year!

RE

REAL EXCELLENCE

JANUARY

RE
REAL EXCELLENCE

JANUARY 1

The Key to Life

Ecclesiastes 7:12 ESV – For the protection of wisdom is like the protection of money, and the advantage of knowledge is that wisdom preserves the life of him who has it.

> Education is the most powerful weapon which you can use to change the world.
>
> ~ Nelson Mandela

REism

Education is a game changer. Continued, ongoing education is the *ultimate* game changer. Always look for ways you can improve and grow intellectually and spiritually.

RE
REAL EXCELLENCE

JANUARY 2

The Price of Your Company

1 Corinthians 15:33 ESV – Do not be deceived: "Bad company ruins good morals."

> Friends and good manners will carry you where money won't go.
>
> ~ Margaret Walker

REism

Be mindful and selective when choosing the company you keep! It's a reflection of you.

MANNERS

RE
REAL EXCELLENCE

JANUARY 3

It's that Time Again:
"I'm getting in shape this year!"

Isaiah 40:28-31 ESV – Have you not known? Have you not heard? The Lord is the everlasting God, the Creator of the ends of the earth. He does not faint or grow weary; his understanding is unsearchable. He gives power to the faint, and to him who has no might he increases strength. Even youths shall faint and be weary, and young men shall fall exhausted; but they who wait for the Lord shall renew their strength; they shall mount up with wings like eagles; they shall run and not be weary; they shall walk and not faint.

> If you don't do what's best for your body, you're the one who comes up on the short end.
>
> ~ Julius Erving

REism

So you hired a personal trainer AGAIN! Note to self: it all starts with YOU! God gives strength to those who seek him daily and believe. Your trainer can only train you if you are committed to the work required. Signing up is just the beginning. Mark this day in your book and use it as a reminder when you get weary.

—— **PHYSICAL ACTIVITY** ——

RE

REAL EXCELLENCE

JANUARY 4

Conflict REsolution

James 3:17 ESV – But the wisdom from above is first pure, then peaceable, gentle, open to reason, full of mercy and good fruits, impartial and sincere.

> Renewal requires opening yourself up to new ways of thinking and feeling.
>
> ~ Deborah Day

REism

The Great Eight Conflict REsolution Process: It works - try it!

Have a Pure Motive, Desire a Peaceful Outcome, Be Gentle in Your Approach, Keep an Open Mind, Be Full of Mercy, Plant Good Fruit, Remain Impartial Throughout and Have a Sincere Heart.

OPEN-MINDEDNESS

JANUARY 5

A Godly Body

1 Corinthians 6:19-20 ESV – Or do you not know that your body is a temple of the Holy Spirit within you, whom you have from God? You are not your own, for you were bought with a price. So glorify God in your body.

Your body is a temple, but only if you treat it as one.

~ Astrid Alauda

REism

Glorify God by taking care of your body.

RE

REAL EXCELLENCE

JANUARY 6

Focus on Solutions

Philippians 2:14-15 ESV – Do all things without grumbling or questioning, that you may be blameless and innocent, children of God without blemish in the midst of a crooked and twisted generation, among whom you shine as lights in the world,

---

We can complain because rose bushes have thorns, or rejoice because thorn bushes have roses.

~ Abraham Lincoln

REism

The REal solution will never be found in a complaint. So stop REstating the problem and REsolve the problem by focusing on solutions!

EXPRESSION OF POSITIVE ATTITUDE

RE
REAL EXCELLENCE

JANUARY 7

UNO

1 Corinthians 13:4-7 ESV – Love is patient and kind; love does not envy or boast; it is not arrogant or rude. It does not insist on its own way; it is not irritable or resentful; it does not rejoice at wrongdoing, but rejoices with the truth. Love bears all things, believes all things, hopes all things, endures all things.

> The consciousness of loving and being loved brings a warmth and richness to life that nothing else can bring.
>
> ~ Oscar Wilde

REism

When I say, "I LOVE YOU", it means you are my UNO = **U**nconditional, **N**ever-ending, **O**xygen for life!

Who is your UNO?

RELATIONSHIPS

JANUARY 8

I'm Covered

Psalm 23:1-6 ESV – A Psalm of David. The Lord is my shepherd; I shall not want. He makes me lie down in green pastures. He leads me beside still waters. He restores my soul. He leads me in paths of righteousness for his name's sake. Even though I walk through the valley of the shadow of death, I will fear no evil, for you are with me; your rod and your staff, they comfort me. You prepare a table before me in the presence of my enemies; you anoint my head with oil; my cup overflows.

> A spirit of gratitude yields patience, love, and forgiveness.
>
> ~ Jarod Kintz

REism

I have unwavering faith in all things because I'm covered by the grace of God!

ENRICHMENT OF SPIRIT

RE

REAL EXCELLENCE

JANUARY 9

Positive Thinking

Romans 12:1-2 ESV – I appeal to you therefore, brothers, by the mercies of God, to present your bodies as a living sacrifice, holy and acceptable to God, which is your spiritual worship. Do not be conformed to this world, but be transformed by the renewal of your mind, that by testing you may discern what is the will of God, what is good and acceptable and perfect.

> What you have to do and the way you have to do it is incredibly simple. Whether you are willing to do it, that's another matter.
>
> ~ Peter F. Drucker

REism

Here's the REality: your thoughts feed your heart, your heart feeds your mind, your mind produces actions, and your actions become your character. Be DEDICATED to positive thinking!

DEDICATION

RE
REAL EXCELLENCE

JANUARY 10

Intentional and Deliberate

Jeremiah 29:11 ESV – For I know the plans I have for you, declares the Lord, plans for welfare and not for evil, to give you a future and a hope.

> Learning is not attained by chance; it must be sought for with ardor and attended to with diligence.
>
> ~ Abigail Adams

REism

The desire to learn is intentional and deliberate!

RE

REAL EXCELLENCE

JANUARY 11

Pay Respect to the Father Every Day

Leviticus 19:32 ESV – You shall stand up before the gray head and honor the face of an old man, and you shall fear your God: I am the Lord.

> God gave you a gift of 84,600 seconds today.
> Have you used one of them to say thank you?
>
> ~ William Arthur Ward

REism

Father, I thank you, for awaking me, and I pray for your blessings today. Amen!

JANUARY 12

Consistency

1 Timothy 4:8 ESV – For while bodily training is of some value, godliness is of value in every way, as it holds promise for the present life and also for the life to come.

> It does not matter how slowly you go as long as you do not stop.
>
> ~ Confucius

REism

Slow and steady has won many races! Stay the course!

JANUARY 13

Seek Wisdom

Proverbs 12:15 ESV – The way of a fool is right in his own eyes, but a wise man listens to advice.

Always be respectful and open-minded when listening to another man's beliefs. What you reject today could be your mantra tomorrow. Man's evolution is all about transformations. An unexpected experience you have one day can change you forever.

~ Suzy Kassem

REism

Seeking the advice of the wise today can pay huge dividends tomorrow.

OPEN-MINDEDNESS

RE

REAL EXCELLENCE

JANUARY 14

Yes, God Created Smoothies Too

Genesis 1:29 ESV – And God said, "Behold, I have given you every plant yielding seed that is on the face of all the earth, and every tree with seed in its fruit. You shall have them for food.

Juices of fruits and vegetables are pure gifts from Mother Nature and the most natural way to heal your body and make yourself whole again.

~ Farnoosh Brock

REism

Be sure to eat a balanced diet daily that includes a smoothie with juice, fruit and vegetables.

WELL-BALANCED NUTRITION

RE
REAL EXCELLENCE

JANUARY 15

REflection

Philippians 4:8-9 ESV – Finally, brothers, whatever is true, whatever is honorable, whatever is just, whatever is pure, whatever is lovely, whatever is commendable, if there is any excellence, if there is anything worthy of praise, think about these things. What you have learned and received and heard and seen in me—practice these things, and the God of peace will be with you.

Cultivate an optimistic mind, use your imagination, always consider alternatives, and dare to believe that you can make possible what others think is impossible.

~ Rodolfo Costa

REism

Find a quiet place and mediate on this scripture. Ask yourself this question: "Are you a positive REflection of God?"

EXPRESSION OF POSITIVE ATTITUDE

JANUARY 16

I DO = ME & YOU not US & THEM

Genesis 2:24 ESV – Therefore a man shall leave his father and his mother and hold fast to his wife, and they shall become one flesh.

> True belonging is born of relationships not only to one another but to a place of shared responsibilities and benefits. We love not so much what we have acquired as what we have made and whom we have made it with.
>
> ~ Robert Finch

REism

We are united as one with the power of two!

RE

REAL EXCELLENCE

JANUARY 17

I'm Praying for You

1 Timothy 2:1-2 ESV – First of all, then, I urge that supplications, prayers, intercessions, and thanksgivings be made for all people, for kings and all who are in high positions, that we may lead a peaceful and quiet life, godly and dignified in every way.

> Great men are they who see that spiritual is stronger than any material force - that thoughts rule the world.
>
> ~ Ralph Waldo Emerson

REism

Praying for others is a good habit. Do you pray for others? How often do you pray for others?

JANUARY 18

All in the Name of Jesus

Colossians 3:17 ESV – And whatever you do, in word or deed, do everything in the name of the Lord Jesus, giving thanks to God the Father through him.

Do all things with love, passion and dedication!

~ Patrick Driessen

REism

Your commitment to Christ is revealed by your daily communication. Walk the walk, and talk the talk!

RE
REAL EXCELLENCE

JANUARY 19

REtention

Proverbs 4:13 ESV – Keep hold of instruction; do not let go; guard her, for she is your life.

> Education is the key to unlock the golden door of freedom.
>
> ~ George Washington Carver

REism

Learn it, apply it, REtain it and REopen it when needed!

RE

REAL EXCELLENCE

JANUARY 20

The Cost is Zero

Proverbs 16:24 ESV – Gracious words are like a honeycomb, sweetness to the soul and health to the body.

> Nothing is ever lost by courtesy. It is the cheapest of the pleasures; costs nothing and conveys much. It pleases him who gives and; him who receives, and thus, like mercy, it is twice blessed.
>
> ~ Erastus Wiman

REism

Acts of kindness will always yield a priceless REturn for those giving and REceiving.

MANNERS

JANUARY 21

Exercising Improves Your Effectiveness

John 1:2 ESV – Beloved, I pray that all may go well with you and that you may be in good health, as it goes well with your soul.

> Physical activity is an excellent stress-buster and provides other health benefits as well. It also can improve your mood and self-image.
>
> ~ Jon Wickham

REism

Daily exercise provides the body with the energy needed to tackle physical and emotional stress. Do you have a daily exercise routine?

PHYSICAL ACTIVITY

RE
REAL EXCELLENCE

JANUARY 22

Are You Willing to Listen?

Proverbs 18:15 ESV – An intelligent heart acquires knowledge, and the ear of the wise seeks knowledge.

> Something interesting happens when we approach situations from a perspective of humility—it opens us up to possibilities as we choose open-mindedness and curiosity over protecting our point of view.
>
> ~ Bruna Martinuzzi

REism

The best strides in life will occur when you realize you don't have all the answers.

OPEN-MINDEDNESS

JANUARY 23

Feed the Tank

Genesis 9:3 ESV – Every moving thing that lives shall be food for you. And as I gave you the green plants, I give you everything.

> Would you pour sand into the gas tank of your car? Of course not, your car was meant to run on good gasoline. Well, your body works the same way. Your body was meant to run on good food: fruits, vegetables, lean protein, and lots of water. Eat good food!
>
> ~ Tom Giaquinto

REism

Food is to the body what gas is to the car. They are both needed to perform.

WELL-BALANCED NUTRITION

RE
REAL EXCELLENCE

JANUARY 24

Who Do You Work For?

Colossians 3:23 ESV – Whatever you do, work heartily, as for the Lord and not for men, knowing that from the Lord you will receive the inheritance as your reward. You are serving the Lord Christ.

God is your Boss! You've got to love that!

~ Tony Dungy

REism

A Godly attitude is always welcome at any place of employment!

EXPRESSION OF POSITIVE ATTITUDE

25

JANUARY 25

Vows REnewed

Psalm 50:14-15 ESV – Offer to God a sacrifice of thanksgiving, and perform your vows to the Most High, and call upon me in the day of trouble; I will deliver you, and you shall glorify me.

> Dreams are renewable. No matter what our age or condition, there are still untapped possibilities within us and new beauty waiting to be born.
>
> ~ Dale E. Turner

REism

It is never too late to REnew your vows.

JANUARY 26

Words Do Hurt

Proverbs 15:1 ESV – A soft answer turns away wrath, but a harsh word stirs up anger.

> If you really want to create peace on the earth, create peace in your heart, in your being. That is the right place to begin with...and then spread and radiate peace and love.
>
> ~ Osho

REism

Let's debunk this age old myth: "Sticks and stones may break my bones, but words will never hurt me." I may have heard that a million times growing up. Well, now that I'm an adult, I know it's far from true. The spoken word can leave the greatest pain!

RE
REAL EXCELLENCE

JANUARY 27

Preparation and Determination

1 Peter 1:13 ESV – Therefore, preparing your minds for action, and being sober-minded, set your hope fully on the grace that will be brought to you at the revelation of Jesus Christ.

> The difference between the impossible and the possible lies in a person's determination.
>
> ~ Tommy Lasorda

REism

Both PREPARATION and DETERMINATION are important factors in regard to accomplishing our goals. But which comes first: Determination or Preparation?

RE

REAL EXCELLENCE

JANUARY 28

Listening

Proverbs 1:5 ESV – Let the wise hear and increase in learning, and the one who understands obtain guidance,

---

Learning is the only thing the mind never exhausts, never fears, and never regrets.

~ Leonardo da Vinci

REism

Listening is the key to expanding your knowledge.

RE
REAL EXCELLENCE

JANUARY 29

Loving Your Brothers and Sisters

Romans 12:10 ESV – Love one another with brotherly affection. Outdo one another in showing honor.

> Good manners will open doors that the best education cannot.
>
> ~ Clarence Thomas

REism

Let your wealth of knowledge lead your actions and interactions with others.

RE

REAL EXCELLENCE

JANUARY 30

Take Action

1 Corinthians 9:27 ESV – But I discipline my body and keep it under control, lest after preaching to others I myself should be disqualified.

> Movement is a medicine for creating change in a person's physical, emotional, and mental states.
>
> ~ Carol Welch

REism

The first step toward better physical fitness is deciding you are not going to stay where you are.

JANUARY 31

An Infinity For God's Word

2 Peter 3:18 ESV – But grow in the grace and knowledge of our Lord and Savior Jesus Christ. To him be the glory both now and to the day of eternity. Amen.

Unless you try to do something beyond what you have already mastered, you will never grow.

~ Ralph Waldo Emerson

REism

The mastering of God's Word has an infinite timeline. Always look for ways you can grow with Christ.

OPEN-MINDEDNESS

FEBRUARY

RE

REAL EXCELLENCE

FEBRUARY 1

Consumption Matters

Proverbs 23:20-21 ESV – Be not among drunkards or among gluttonous eaters of meat, for the drunkard and the glutton will come to poverty, and slumber will clothe them with rags.

> The spirit cannot endure the body when overfed, but, if underfed, the body cannot endure the spirit.
>
> ~ St Frances de Sales

REism

A diet that features moderate portions and a sober desire will yield the body a great REturn.

RE
REAL EXCELLENCE

FEBRUARY 2

Your Best Work

1 Peter 3:15 ESV – but in your hearts honor Christ the Lord as holy, always being prepared to make a defense to anyone who asks you for a reason for the hope that is in you; yet do it with gentleness and respect

> It's so hard when I have to, and so easy when I want to.
>
> ~ Annie Gottlier

REism

A servant and willing heart performs his or her best work.

RE
REAL EXCELLENCE

FEBRUARY 3

Judgement Day

Hebrews 9:27 ESV – And just as it is appointed for man to die once, and after that comes judgment,

---

> A good character is the best tombstone. Those who loved you and were helped by you will remember you when forget-me-nots have withered. Carve your name on hearts, not on marble.
>
> ~ Charles H. Spurgeon

REism

This may be an uncomfortable question, but one you should ask yourself: "If God called you home today, what would your tombstone read?"

RELATIONSHIPS

FEBRUARY 4

The Flesh vs The Spirit

Romans 8:13-14 ESV – For if you live according to the flesh you will die, but if by the Spirit you put to death the deeds of the body, you will live. For all who are led by the Spirit of God are sons of God.

> The spiritual life does not remove us from the world but leads us deeper into it.
>
> ~ Henri J.M. Nouwen

REism

Affirmation: I will live by the Spirit of God, so my life is a beam of light for the world.

REAL EXCELLENCE

FEBRUARY 5

The Pain of Discipline

Hebrews 12:11 ESV – For the moment all discipline seems painful rather than pleasant, but later it yields the peaceful fruit of righteousness to those who have been trained by it.

> Discipline is the foundation upon which all success is built.
>
> ~ Jim Rohn

REism

A lack of discipline inadvertently leads to procrastination, failure and regret. How is your discipline?

DEDICATION

FEBRUARY 6

Doors Wide Open

Isaiah 28:9-10 ESV – To whom will he teach knowledge, and to whom will he explain the message? Those who are weaned from the milk, those taken from the breast? For it is precept upon precept, precept upon precept, line upon line, line upon line, here a little, there a little.

Education's purpose is to replace an empty mind with an open one.

~ Malcolm Forbes

REism

Knock, Knock.
Who's there?
Knowledge!
Come on in, Knowledge. I'm ready.

EDUCATION

RE
REAL EXCELLENCE

FEBRUARY 7

Showing Appreciation

Proverbs 23:1 ESV – When you sit down to eat with a ruler, observe carefully what is before you,

---

Gratitude is the most exquisite form of courtesy.

~ Jacques Maritain

REism

Your company will remember how you made them feel long after the food digests. A simple "please" and "thank you" will never be forgotten.

MANNERS

RE

REAL EXCELLENCE

FEBRUARY 8

Looking Good

Proverbs 31:17 ESV – She dresses herself with strength and makes her arms strong.

To enjoy the glow of good health, you must exercise.

~ Gene Tunney

REism

I'm feeling even better, because I couldn't fit into this dress a month ago! Exercising is great! Are you committed, or is it time to REcommit?

PHYSICAL ACTIVITY

RE

REAL EXCELLENCE

FEBRUARY 9

Pressing the RElease Button

Luke 24:45 ESV – Then he opened their minds to understand the Scriptures,

---

Minds are like parachutes. They only function when open.

~ Thomas Dewar

REism

Having a closed mind is like jumping out of an aircraft and not using your parachute.

OPEN-MINDEDNESS

FEBRUARY 10

Spiritual Feeding

John 6:35 ESV – Jesus said to them, "I am the bread of life; whoever comes to me shall not hunger, and whoever believes in me shall never thirst.

> Just imagine, how much easier our lives
> would be if we were born with a 'user guide
> or owner's manual' which could tell us what
> to eat and how to live healthy.
>
> ~ Erika M. Szabo

REism

The Bible's spiritual feeding should be done daily.

WELL-BALANCED NUTRITION

RE

REAL EXCELLENCE

FEBRUARY 11

The Beehive

Proverbs 17:22 ESV – A joyful heart is good medicine, but a crushed spirit dries up the bones.

Life is simple. Your life is made up of only two kinds of things – positive things and negative things.

~ Rhonda Byrne

REism

Catch the beehive of POSITIVE THINGS with a spirit full of honey.

RE
REAL EXCELLENCE

FEBRUARY 12

A Receive and Give Relationship

2 Corinthians 5:17 ESV – Therefore, if anyone is in Christ, he is a new creation. The old has passed away; behold, the new has come.

> The process of really being with other people in a safe, supportive situation can actually change who we think we are. . . . And as we grow closer to the essence of who we are, we tend to take more responsibility for our neighbors and our planet.
>
> ~ Bill Kauth

REism

With more blessings come more responsibility. Christ wants His disciples to look for ways to increase their territory.

RELATIONSHIPS

FEBRUARY 13

Look Up!

1 Corinthians 2:1-5 ESV – And I, when I came to you, brothers, did not come proclaiming to you the testimony of God with lofty speech or wisdom. For I decided to know nothing among you except Jesus Christ and him crucified. And I was with you in weakness and in fear and much trembling, and my speech and my message were not in plausible words of wisdom, but in demonstration of the Spirit and of power, that your faith might not rest in the wisdom of men but in the power of God.

> The human spirit is stronger than anything that can happen to it.
>
> ~ C.C. Scott

REism

God's strength is the perfect example of the strength needed to endure a broken spirit and to REjoice in a joyful spirit.

If your spirits are low, look up and smile because God loves you!

If your spirits are high, look up and say, "Thank you God for blessing me!"

ENRICHMENT OF SPIRIT

RE
REAL EXCELLENCE

FEBRUARY 14

Keeping Your Eyes On The Prize

Psalm 1:1-6 ESV – Blessed is the man who walks not in the counsel of the wicked, nor stands in the way of sinners, nor sits in the seat of scoffers; but his delight is in the law of the Lord, and on his law he meditates day and night. He is like a tree planted by streams of water that yields its fruit in its season, and its leaf does not wither. In all that he does, he prospers. The wicked are not so, but are like chaff that the wind drives away. Therefore the wicked will not stand in the judgment, nor sinners in the congregation of the righteous; ...

> To succeed in your mission, you must have single-minded devotion to your goal.
>
> ~ A. P. J. Abdul Kalam

REism

How do you keep your eyes on the prize? FOCUS! Follow One Course Until Successful.

───────────── **DEDICATION** ─────────────

RE

REAL EXCELLENCE

FEBRUARY 15

Education Has No Finish Line

Psalm 32:8 ESV – I will instruct you and teach you in the way you should go; I will counsel you with my eye upon you.

Let us never be betrayed into saying we have finished our education; because that would mean we had stopped growing.

~ Julia H. Gulliver

REism

If learning was a race, all the winners would never finish! There is always room for growth.

RE
REAL EXCELLENCE

FEBRUARY 16

Humility

Philippians 2:3 ESV – Do nothing from rivalry or conceit, but in humility count others more significant than yourselves.

> Let not a man guard his dignity, but let his dignity guard him.
>
> ~ Ralph Waldo Emerson

REism

Humility is not thinking less of yourself, it is thinking of yourself less.

MANNERS

RE

REAL EXCELLENCE

FEBRUARY 17

Who Are You Racing?

2 Chronicles 20:15 ESV – Do not be afraid and do not be dismayed at this great horde, for the battle is not yours but God's.

> If you fall behind, run faster. Never give up, never surrender, and rise up against the odds.
>
> ~ Jesse Jackson

REism

If you are in a race with Satan, REmove yourself from that race with spiritual conditioning and join The REal race with God.

PHYSICAL ACTIVITY

RE
REAL EXCELLENCE

FEBRUARY 18

Tunnel Vision

Proverbs 16:25 ESV – There is a way that seems right to a man, but its end is the way to death.

> The most fatal illusion is the settled point of view. Since life is growth and motion, a fixed point of view kills anybody who has one.
>
> ~ Brooks Atkinson

REism

When seeking the truth go to the Word. It is the answer key to all of life's test questions.

OPEN-MINDEDNESS

RE

REAL EXCELLENCE

FEBRUARY 19

From the Inside Out

Matthew 3:8 ESV – Bear fruit in keeping with repentance.

> A healthy outside starts from the inside.
>
> ~ Robert Urich

REism

A well-fed body rejects bad food and disposes of it because it is useless.

Are you eating right?

RE

REAL EXCELLENCE

FEBRUARY 20

Good Fortune

Colossians 3:10 ESV – And have put on the new self, which is being renewed in knowledge after the image of its creator.

> Henceforth I ask not good-fortune, I myself am good-fortune.
>
> ~ Walt Whitman

REism

Once God's spirit takes over, your REnewed attitude is one of good fortune.

EXPRESSION OF POSITIVE ATTITUDE

53

RE

REAL EXCELLENCE

FEBRUARY 21

A Two Way Street

Genesis 2:18 ESV – Then the Lord God said, "It is not good that the man should be alone; I will make him a helper fit for him."

> You can't have community as an add-on to a monetized life. You have to actually need each other.
>
> ~ Charles Eisenstein

REism

I scratch your back, you scratch my back, and together we are made whole.

RE
REAL EXCELLENCE

FEBRUARY 22

Forgiveness

Romans 3:23 ESV – For all have sinned and fall short of the glory of God,

---

Make peace with yourself, and both heaven and earth will make peace with you.

~ Isaac of Nineveh

REism

The ability to forgive others starts with the ability to forgive yourself. Your past mishaps are not a place of residence. Press forward and learn from your past experiences.

RE

FEBRUARY 23

Defeating Obstacles Along The Way

Philippians 3:8-11 ESV – Indeed, I count everything as loss because of the surpassing worth of knowing Christ Jesus my Lord. For his sake I have suffered the loss of all things and count them as rubbish, in order that I may gain Christ and be found in him, not having a righteousness of my own that comes from the law, but that which comes through faith in Christ, the righteousness from God that depends on faith— that I may know him and the power of his resurrection, and may share his sufferings, becoming like him in his death, that by any means possible I may attain the resurrection from the dead.

> Brick walls are there for a reason. They give us a chance to show how badly we want something.
>
> ~ Randy Pausch

REism

Becoming more deeply and emotionally attached to God will provide the strength, power and determination you need to defeat all of life's obstacles.

—————————— **DEDICATION** ——————————

RE
REAL EXCELLENCE

FEBRUARY 24

Transparency

Deuteronomy 28:13 ESV – And the Lord will make you the head and not the tail, and you shall only go up and not down, if you obey the commandments of the Lord your God, which I command you today, being careful to do them,

---

> The function of education is to teach one to think intensively and to think critically. Intelligence plus character--that is the goal of true education.
>
> ~ Martin Luther King, Jr.

REism

Transparent leadership is one of good moral character and gives its followers reason to trust and believe in the destination.

EDUCATION

RE

REAL EXCELLENCE

FEBRUARY 25

Encouragement Needed

Ephesians 4:29 ESV – Let no corrupting talk come out of your mouths, but only such as is good for building up, as fits the occasion, that it may give grace to those who hear.

> All doors open to courtesy.
>
> ~ Thomas Fuller

REism

Be an 'encourager' today. Pick out three people in your circle and drop them an encouraging note. You will be surprised what an uplifting note does for a person's confidence.

MANNERS

RE

REAL EXCELLENCE

FEBRUARY 26

A Rare Commodity

1 Corinthians 6:19-20 ESV – Or do you not know that your body is a temple of the Holy Spirit within you, whom you have from God? You are not your own, for you were bought with a price. So glorify God in your body.

> Take care of your body. It's the only place you have to live.
>
> ~ Jim Rohn

REism

Your body is a precious gift from God and should be taken care of like the rare commodity it is.

RE
REAL EXCELLENCE

FEBRUARY 27

Creative Thinking

Isaiah 43:18-19 ESV – Remember not the former things, nor consider the things of old. Behold, I am doing a new thing; now it springs forth, do you not perceive it? I will make a way in the wilderness and rivers in the desert.

> You can teach a student a lesson for a day; but if you can teach him to learn by creating curiosity, he will continue the learning process as long as he lives.
>
> ~ Clay P. Bedford

REism

Daring to be different has led to some of our greatest inventions and success stories.

OPEN-MINDEDNESS

FEBRUARY 28/29

Veggies Matter

Daniel 1:11-16 ESV – Then Daniel said to the steward whom the chief of the eunuchs had assigned over Daniel, Hananiah, Mishael, and Azariah, "Test your servants for ten days; let us be given vegetables to eat and water to drink. Then let our appearance and the appearance of the youths who eat the king's food be observed by you, and deal with your servants according to what you see." So he listened to them in this matter, and tested them for ten days. At the end of ten days it was seen that they were better in appearance and fatter in flesh than all the youths who ate the king's food...

> Beauty isn't something on the outside. It's your insides that count! You gotta eat green stuff to make sure you're pretty on the inside.
>
> ~ Takayuki Ikkaku

REism

Are your vegetables complementing your diet?

WELL-BALANCED NUTRITION

MARCH

RE
REAL EXCELLENCE

MARCH 1

You Control the Temperature

Philippians 2:5 ESV – Have this mind among yourselves, which is yours in Christ Jesus,

> The only difference between a good day and a bad day is your attitude.
>
> ~ Dennis S. Brown

REism

Your attitude is like a thermostat that you control. You should always be in complete control of the temperature in your room.

RE

REAL EXCELLENCE

MARCH 2

No Need, No Want, No Desire, Not Even a Wandering Eye

Matthew 5:27-28 ESV – You have heard that it was said, "You shall not commit adultery." But I say to you that everyone who looks at a woman with lustful intent has already committed adultery with her in his heart.

Love is a game that only two can play and both win.

~ Eva Gabor

REism

I Only Have Eyes For My UNO! No third party allowed! This domain is reserved for My UNO and me.

RELATIONSHIPS

RE

REAL EXCELLENCE

MARCH 3

Electricity

John 14:6 ESV – Jesus said to him, "I am the way, and the truth, and the life. No one comes to the Father except through me."

Just as a candle cannot burn without fire,
men cannot live without a spiritual life.

~ Buddha

REism

Jesus is the electricity that lights our soul.

MARCH 4

The Motivation of Music

Nehemiah 12:27 ESV – And at the dedication of the wall of Jerusalem they sought the Levites in all their places, to bring them to Jerusalem to celebrate the dedication with gladness, with thanksgivings and with singing, with cymbals, harps, and lyres.

Dedication means spending whatever time or energy is necessary to accomplish the task at hand.

~ Anil Sinha

REism

Your celebration happens on the other side of hard work and should come with victory music.

What is your victory music selection? Use music as an inspiration.

DEDICATION

MARCH 5

Learning Helps Your Decision Making

1 Corinthians 10:29 ESV – I do not mean your conscience, but his. For why should my liberty be determined by someone else's conscience?

Next in importance to freedom and justice is popular education, without which neither freedom nor justice can be maintained.

~ James A. Garfield

REism

The uneducated mind is a slave to his or her surroundings and will be held hostage by the thoughts and decisions of others. Information learned helps our ability to think and make decisions.

EDUCATION

MARCH 6

Reciprocated Behavior

1 Corinthians 13:4-5 ESV – Love is patient and kind; love does not envy or boast; it is not arrogant or rude. It does not insist on its own way; it is not irritable or resentful;

> He who sows courtesy reaps friendship, and he who plants kindness gathers love.
>
> ~ St. Basil

REism

Be kind and friendly to others, and you will receive kindness and friendliness in return.

RE
REAL EXCELLENCE

MARCH 7

Body and Soul

Proverbs 24:5 ESV – A wise man is full of strength, and a man of knowledge enhances his might,

---

> Exercise should be regarded as tribute to the heart.
>
> ~ Gene Tunney

REism

Training your body will yield great strength, but training your heart as well will give your soul the full armor of strength needed to endure all things.

MARCH 8

The Exploratory Mind of a Child

Exodus 36:1 ESV – Bezalel and Oholiab and every craftsman in whom the Lord has put skill and intelligence to know how to do any work in the construction of the sanctuary shall work in accordance with all that the Lord has commanded.

If we maintain the open-mindedness of children, we challenge fixed ideas and established structures, including our own.

~ Brennan Manning

REism

A child-like curiosity and an educated Godly craftsman can open the mind to doors of untapped potential.

Tap into your fountain of youth!

OPEN-MINDEDNESS

RE
REAL EXCELLENCE

MARCH 9

Bad Habits Become Toxic

Proverbs 30:8-9 ESV – Remove far from me falsehood and lying; give me neither poverty nor riches; feed me with the food that is needful for me, lest I be full and deny you and say, "Who is the Lord?" or lest I be poor and steal and profane the name of my God.

> No single food will make or break good health. But the kinds of food you choose day in and day out have a major impact.
>
> ~ Walter Willet

REism

You can overcome missing a church service, bible class, book club reading or fellowship group meeting here or there. Just don't make it habit! A healthy diet can overcome a bad meal here or there; however, if you make a habit of eating poorly, it will become toxic to your body.

WELL-BALANCED NUTRITION

RE

REAL EXCELLENCE

MARCH 10

Value Your Energy

Psalm 150:1-6 ESV – Praise the Lord! Praise God in his sanctuary; praise him in his mighty heavens! Praise him for his mighty deeds; praise him according to his excellent greatness! Praise him with trumpet sound; praise him with lute and harp! Praise him with tambourine and dance; praise him with strings and pipe! Praise him with sounding cymbals; praise him with loud clashing cymbals! ...

> Happiness is an attitude. We either make ourselves miserable, or happy and strong. The amount of work is the same.
>
> ~ Francesca Reigler

REism

How are you using your energy? Is it having an impact on your life?

MARCH 11

Oil and Water

2 Corinthians 6:14 ESV – Do not be unequally yoked with unbelievers. For what partnership has righteousness with lawlessness? Or what fellowship has light with darkness?

> Relation is the essence of everything that exists.
>
> ~ Meister Eckhart

REism

Try mixing oil and water and see what you get.

MARCH 12

Leaving a Legacy

Mark 10:17-21 ESV – And as he was setting out on his journey, a man ran up and knelt before him and asked him, "Good Teacher, what must I do to inherit eternal life?" And Jesus said to him, "Why do you call me good? No one is good except God alone. You know the commandments: 'Do not murder, Do not commit adultery, Do not steal, Do not bear false witness, Do not defraud, Honor your father and mother.'" And he said to him, "Teacher, all these I have kept from my youth." And Jesus, looking at him, loved him, and said to him, "You lack one thing: go, sell all that you have and give to the poor, and you will have treasure in heaven; and come, follow me."

> Remember that when you leave this earth, you can take with you nothing that you have received-only what you have given: a full heart enriched by honest service, love, sacrifice and courage.
>
> ~ Saint Francis of Assisi

REism

Everything you do for yourself will die with you, but everything you do for others will live forever.

ENRICHMENT OF SPIRIT

MARCH 13

See No Evil, Believe No Evil

James 1:2-4 ESV – Count it all joy, my brothers, when you meet trials of various kinds, for you know that the testing of your faith produces steadfastness. And let steadfastness have its full effect, that you may be perfect and complete, lacking in nothing.

> Obstacles are those frightful things you see when you take your eyes off your goal.
>
> ~ Henry Ford

REism

Don't allow your eyes to send unwanted messages to your soul.

DEDICATION

MARCH 14

Applying Your Knowledge

Proverbs 23:12 ESV – Apply your heart to instruction and your ear to words of knowledge.

> Education, like the mass of our age's inventions, is after all, only a tool; everything depends upon the workman who uses it.
>
> ~ Charles Wagner, *The Simple Life*

REism

Application is the definition of learning.

RE
REAL EXCELLENCE

MARCH 15

Parental Guidance

Titus 3:2 ESV – To speak evil of no one, to avoid quarreling, to be gentle, and to show perfect courtesy toward all people.

> Be kind whenever possible. It is always possible.
>
> ~ Tenzin Gyatso

REism

Your parents always said, "If you don't have anything nice to say, don't say anything at all." Be uplifting, it's what your parents advised.

MANNERS

RE

MARCH 16

You Must Believe

Philippians 4:13 ESV – I can do all things through him who strengthens me.

A feeble body weakens the mind.

~ Jean-Jacques Rousseau

REism

The body can't achieve what the mind can't conceive. Own it, Work it, and You will Become it!

PHYSICAL ACTIVITY

RE
REAL EXCELLENCE

MARCH 17

Core Beliefs

Hosea 6:6 ESV – For I desire steadfast love and not sacrifice, the knowledge of God rather than burnt offerings.

> A person with a fixed idea will always find some way of convincing himself in the end that he is right.
>
> ~ Atle Selberg

REism

Be very careful with what you believe in, because our decisions are heavily based on our core beliefs.

Affirmation: I will lean on God for my core beliefs and guidance with my decisions.

OPEN-MINDEDNESS

MARCH 18

How Important are YOU to YOU?

1 Corinthians 10:25 ESV – Eat whatever is sold in the meat market without raising any question on the ground of conscience.

> You are what you eat. What would YOU like to be?
>
> ~ Julie Murphy

REism

If you are important enough to yourself, YOU will be very conscience about what YOU eat.

Your body is your temple!

RE
REAL EXCELLENCE

MARCH 19

Bucket Filler or Bucket Dipper

Matthew 5:2-4 ESV – And he opened his mouth and taught them, saying:

Blessed are the poor in spirit, for theirs is the kingdom of heaven.

Blessed are those who mourn, for they shall be comforted.

> Your choices of action may be limited, but your choices of thought are not.
>
> ~ Abraham–Hicks

REism

Bucket Fillers are always looking for ways to lift up others and add value to the bucket.

Bucket Dippers are always looking for ways to extract from the bucket and put others down.

Are you a Bucket Filler or Bucket Dipper?

EXPRESSION OF POSITIVE ATTITUDE

RE
REAL EXCELLENCE

MARCH 20

Character Counts and Make Up Matters

1 Timothy 3:4-7 ESV – He must manage his own household well, with all dignity keeping his children submissive, for if someone does not know how to manage his own household, how will he care for God's church? He must not be a recent convert, or he may become puffed up with conceit and fall into the condemnation of the devil. Moreover, he must be well thought of by outsiders, so that he may not fall into disgrace, into a snare of the devil.

> Each of us must rededicate ourselves to serving the common good. We are a community. Our individual Fates are linked; our futures intertwined; and if we act in that knowledge and in that spirit together, as the Bible says: "We can move mountains."
>
> ~ Jimmy Carter

REism

A leader's relationship with those he or she is leading will always be impacted by their view of his or her character traits. A well-regarded leader can accomplish what others view as impossible.

RELATIONSHIPS

MARCH 21

Planting Seeds Along Your Path

Matthew 13:1-58 ESV – That same day Jesus went out of the house and sat beside the sea. And great crowds gathered about him, so that he got into a boat and sat down. And the whole crowd stood on the beach. And he told them many things in parables, saying: "A sower went out to sow. And as he sowed, some seeds fell along the path, and the birds came and devoured them. Other seeds fell on rocky ground, where they did not have much soil, and immediately they sprang up, since they had no depth of soil, ...

> Impart as much as you can of your spiritual being to those who are on the road with you, and accept as something precious what comes back to you from them.
>
> ~ Albert Schweitzer

REism

You should always look for an opportunity to grow your territory.

RE

REAL EXCELLENCE

MARCH 22

Aim to Please God

1 Corinthians 2:9-10 ESV – But, as it is written, "What no eye has seen, nor ear heard, nor the heart of man imagined, what God has prepared for those who love him"— these things God has revealed to us through the Spirit. For the Spirit searches everything, even the depths of God."

Above all be of single aim; have a legitimate and useful purpose, and devote yourself unreservedly to it.

~ James Allen

REism

I am Dedicated to God, and only God, and that decision is without reservation.

MARCH 23

The Stakes are High

Proverbs 9:9-10 ESV – Give instruction to a wise man, and he will be still wiser; teach a righteous man, and he will increase in learning. The fear of the Lord is the beginning of wisdom, and the knowledge of the Holy One is insight.

> Upon the education of the people of this country, the fate of this country depends.
>
> ~ Benjamin Disraeli

REism

Looking out for others is admirable, but there is a lot riding on how well we educate our own.

EDUCATION

MARCH 24

You Said It and You Must Own It

Matthew 15:11 ESV – It is not what goes into the mouth that defiles a person, but what comes out of the mouth; this defiles a person.

> Good manners and soft words have brought many a difficult thing to pass.
>
> ~ Sir John Vanbrugh

REism

The spoken word can never be retracted, so choose your words wisely.

RE
REAL EXCELLENCE

MARCH 25

An Opportunity For God?

2 Corinthians 12:9 ESV – But he said to me, "My grace is sufficient for you, for my power is made perfect in weakness." Therefore I will boast all the more gladly of my weaknesses, so that the power of Christ may rest upon me.

> Take care of your body with steadfast fidelity. The soul must see through these eyes alone, and if they are dim, the whole world is clouded.
>
> ~ Johann Wolfgang von Goethe

REism

Human weakness is no stranger to God. It is His opportunity to reveal His strength and power. In your weakness you are made strong by the power of God.

PHYSICAL ACTIVITY

RE
REAL EXCELLENCE

MARCH 26

Open to the Truth

1 John 5:20 ESV – And we know that the Son of God has come and has given us understanding, so that we may know him who is true; and we are in him who is true, in his Son Jesus Christ. He is the true God and eternal life.

> If someone is able to show me that what I think or do is not right, I will happily change, for I seek the truth, by which no one was ever truly harmed. It is the person who continues in his self-deception and ignorance who is harmed.
>
> ~ Marcus Aurelius

REism

Be confident not in yourself, but in Christ who dwells in you. Satan will try to steal your confidence, but you must remain steadfast to the undeniable truth.

OPEN-MINDEDNESS

RE
REAL EXCELLENCE

MARCH 27

Private to Public

Proverbs 23:20 ESV – Be not among drunkards or among gluttonous eaters of meat,

---

One should eat to live, not live to eat.

~ Moliere

REism

What you eat in private, you wear in public!

RE
REAL EXCELLENCE

MARCH 28

Let God Lead The Way

James 4:10 ESV – Humble yourselves before the Lord, and he will exalt you.

Cultivate an optimistic mind, use your imagination, always consider alternatives, and dare to believe that you can make possible what others think is impossible.

~ Rodolfo Costa

REism

Trust God and recognize that He is greater than you in every way. Your job is to listen to God and let Him lead the way.

EXPRESSION OF POSITIVE ATTITUDE

RE

REAL EXCELLENCE

MARCH 29

I'm Your Number One Supporter

1 Thessalonians 5:11 ESV – Therefore encourage one another and build one another up, just as you are doing.

> Without a sense of caring, there can be no sense of community.
>
> ~ Anthony J. D'Angelo

REism

Don't assume they know. You must speak it, show it, be a sounding board, a voice of reason and an advisor.

RELATIONSHIPS

MARCH 30

God's Will

1 John 2:1-5 ESV – My little children, I am writing these things to you so that you may not sin. But if anyone does sin, we have an advocate with the Father, Jesus Christ the righteous. He is the propitiation for our sins, and not for ours only but also for the sins of the whole world. And by this we know that we have come to know him, if we keep his commandments. Whoever says "I know him" but does not keep his commandments is a liar, and the truth is not in him, but whoever keeps his word, in him truly the love of God is perfected. By this we may know that we are in him:

> Soul development should take precedence over all things.
>
> ~ Edgar Cay

REism

To release the full power of the Holy Spirit within you, you must allow God's Will to be done, knowing that everything in your life will change.

ENRICHMENT OF SPIRIT

RE
REAL EXCELLENCE

MARCH 31

Our Steps Are Ordered

Revelation 14:12 ESV – Here is a call for the endurance of the saints, those who keep the commandments of God and their faith in Jesus.

> When the will is ready the feet are light.
>
> ~ Proverb

REism

Your dedicated walk of blind faith has you ready to walk and be a light for God.

RE

REAL EXCELLENCE

APRIL

RE
REAL EXCELLENCE

APRIL 1

Access to Freedom

Romans 12:2 ESV – Do not be conformed to this world, but be transformed by the renewal of your mind, that by testing you may discern what is the will of God, what is good and acceptable and perfect.

> Only the educated are free.
>
> ~ Epictetus

REism

In order for God to free your soul, you must allow God to transform your mind.

APRIL 2

Are You Keeping Company With Non-Believers?

1 John 4:5-6 ESV – They are from the world; therefore they speak from the world, and the world listens to them. We are from God. Whoever knows God listens to us; whoever is not from God does not listen to us. By this we know the Spirit of truth and the spirit of error.

A man's manners are a mirror in which he shows his portrait.

~ Johann Wolfgang von Goethe

REism

Make sure your portrait stays the same regardless of the company. You are in the world, not of the world.

MANNERS

RE

REAL EXCELLENCE

APRIL 3

The Total Package

1 Peter 3:3-4 ESV – Do not let your adorning be external—the braiding of hair and the putting on of gold jewelry, or the clothing you wear—but let your adorning be the hidden person of the heart with the imperishable beauty of a gentle and quiet spirit, which in God's sight is very precious.

> The reason I exercise is for the quality of life I enjoy.
>
> ~ Kenneth H. Cooper

REism

Exercise can improve your outward appearance—the things that people see. But your inner life is what you do to honor the Lord.

Are you the total package?

PHYSICAL ACTIVITY

RE

REAL EXCELLENCE

APRIL 4

Open Flame of Fire

Colossians 1:10 ESV – So as to walk in a manner worthy of the Lord, fully pleasing to him, bearing fruit in every good work and increasing in the knowledge of God.

> The understanding is not a vessel which must be filled, but firewood, which needs to be kindled; and love of learning and love of truth are what should kindle it.
>
> ~ Plutarch

REism

Look for ways to constantly add wood to your fire of knowledge.

APRIL 5

Everybody is an Artist

Deuteronomy 8:3 ESV – And he humbled you and let you hunger and fed you with manna, which you did not know, nor did your fathers know, that he might make you know that man does not live by bread alone, but man lives by every word that comes from the mouth of the Lord.

> To eat is a necessity, but to eat intelligently is an art.
>
> ~ La Rochefoucauld

REism

Your diet will paint a picture of your outward body. Make sure you approve of the artwork.

WELL-BALANCED NUTRITION

RE
REAL EXCELLENCE

APRIL 6

Math is Life

Colossians 3:17 ESV – And whatever you do, in word or deed, do everything in the name of the Lord Jesus, giving thanks to God the Father through him.

Virtually nothing is impossible in this world if you just put your mind to it and maintain a positive attitude.

~ Lou Holtz

REism

Life is a math equation. To get the best REsults, you have to know how to turn negatives into positives.

EXPRESSION OF POSITIVE ATTITUDE

APRIL 7

Keeping The Water Out of The Boat

2 Samuel 22:31 ESV – This God—his way is perfect; the word of the Lord proves true; he is a shield for all those who take refuge in him.

Strange is our situation here upon earth. Each of us comes for a short visit, not knowing why, yet sometimes seeming to divine a purpose. From the standpoint of daily life, however, there is one thing we do know: that man is here for the sake of other men.

~ Albert Einstein

REism

Imagine your relationship with God is like being on a boat. A boat doesn't sink because it is in the water; it sinks because the water gets into the boat. Christians don't fail to live as they should because they are in the world; they fail because they allow the world to live in them.

———— RELATIONSHIPS ————

RE
REAL EXCELLENCE

APRIL 8

The Spirit Flame

1 Peter 2:1-5 ESV – So put away all malice and all deceit and hypocrisy and envy and all slander. Like newborn infants, long for the pure spiritual milk, that by it you may grow up into salvation— if indeed you have tasted that the Lord is good. As you come to him, a living stone rejected by men but in the sight of God chosen and precious, you yourselves like living stones are being built up as a spiritual house, to be a holy priesthood, to offer spiritual sacrifices acceptable to God through Jesus Christ.

> Knowledge without Spirit is like finding yourself on a cold night with all the wood in the world and no flame to ignite it.
>
> ~ Guy Finley

REism

Are you just a bunch of wood, or is your flame ignited?

ENRICHMENT OF SPIRIT

RE

REAL EXCELLENCE

APRIL 9

Put It On His Shoulders

1 Peter 1:8 ESV – Though you have not seen him, you love him. Though you do not now see him, you believe in him and rejoice with joy that is inexpressible and filled with glory,

> The world makes way for the man who knows where he is going.
>
> ~ Ralph Waldo Emerson

REism

When you are dedicated to being in full partnership with God, He can shoulder the heaviness of the burden and provide wisdom, power and protection.

APRIL 10

Avoid The Hollow Vessel Syndrome

Proverbs 16:16 ESV – How much better to get wisdom than gold! To get understanding is to be chosen rather than silver.

> Education is the kindling of a flame, not the filling of a vessel.
>
> ~ Socrates

REism

Education is best served when used to inspire others for God's glory.

RE
REAL EXCELLENCE

APRIL 11

Edifying One Another

1 Thessalonians 5:11 ESV – Therefore encourage one another and build one another up, just as you are doing.

> Wherever there is a human being, there is an opportunity for a kindness.
>
> ~ Seneca

REism

You were created to make someone else's life better. Somebody needs what you have—your smile, your love and your encouragement.

APRIL 12

Paying The Price

Romans 12:1 ESV – I appeal to you therefore, brothers, by the mercies of God, to present your bodies as a living sacrifice, holy and acceptable to God, which is your spiritual worship.

> Physical fitness is not only one of the most important keys to a healthy body, it is the basis of dynamic and creative intellectual activity.
>
> ~ John F. Kennedy

REism

There is a price to be paid for good physical health.

Are you willing to pay the price?

PHYSICAL ACTIVITY

RE
REAL EXCELLENCE

APRIL 13

Letting Go of Preconceived Notions

John 16:23 ESV – In that day you will ask nothing of me. Truly, truly, I say to you, whatever you ask of the Father in my name, he will give it to you.

Sit down before fact with an open mind. Be prepared to give up every preconceived notion. Follow humbly wherever and to whatever abyss Nature leads or you learn nothing.

~ Hyman G. Rickover

REism

When asking, you must give up all preconceived notions, be patient and have complete trust in His answer.

OPEN-MINDEDNESS

APRIL 14

Read The Nutritional Facts On The Label

Leviticus 11:1-4 ESV – And the Lord spoke to Moses and Aaron, saying to them, "Speak to the people of Israel, saying, These are the living things that you may eat among all the animals that are on the earth. Whatever parts the hoof and is cloven-footed and chews the cud, among the animals, you may eat. Nevertheless, among those that chew the cud or part the hoof, you shall not eat these: The camel, because it chews the cud but does not part the hoof, is unclean to you.

> The food you eat can be either the safest and most powerful form of medicine or the slowest form of poison.
>
> ~ Ann Wigmore

REism

All food is not good food! Some foods taste good to you, but are bad for you. Do your REsearch!

WELL-BALANCED NUTRITION

RE
REAL EXCELLENCE

APRIL 15

How High Do You Want To Go?

Psalm 139:14 ESV – I praise you, for I am fearfully and wonderfully made. Wonderful are your works; my soul knows it very well.

> Attitude is a little thing that makes a big difference.
>
> ~ Winston Churchill

REism

Your attitude will determine your altitude.

RE

REAL EXCELLENCE

APRIL 16

Loving Your Fellow Brother and Sister

1 John 4:11 ESV – Beloved, if God so loved us, we also ought to love one another.

Be fair. Treat the other man as you would be treated.

~ Everett W. Lord

REism

Ask yourself, "How would I want to be treated?" Then treat your brother and sister in that way.

APRIL 17

A Thankful Spirit

Colossians 3:15 ESV – And let the peace of Christ rule in your hearts, to which indeed you were called in one body. And be thankful.

> Gratitude unlocks the fullness of life. It turns what we have into enough, and more. It can turn a meal into a feast, a house into a home, a stranger into a friend.
>
> ~ Melody Beattie

REism

When was the last time you thanked Christ for all He has done for you?

Thank Him today!

RE
REAL EXCELLENCE

APRIL 18

Confidence Booster

Psalm 32:8 ESV – I will instruct you and teach you in the way you should go; I will counsel you with my eye upon you.

Confidence doesn't come out of nowhere. It's a result of something... hours and days and weeks and years of constant work and dedication.

~ Roger Staubach

REism

Don't be surprised when you are rewarded for your dedication to Him. God's power is unlimited!

DEDICATION

RE

REAL EXCELLENCE

APRIL 19

Mentorship

Proverbs 27:17 ESV – Iron sharpens iron, and one man sharpens another.

> Education is simply the soul of a society as it passes from one generation to another.
>
> ~ G. K. Chesterton

REism

The sharing of knowledge is the best way to assure your legacy will live forever.

Are you currently mentoring anyone? If so, keep doing God's Work and He will continue to bless you.

If not, get started today!

EDUCATION

RE

REAL EXCELLENCE

APRIL 20

Avoid The Sour Taste of Vinegar

Proverbs 18:20 ESV – From the fruit of a man's mouth his stomach is satisfied; he is satisfied by the yield of his lips.

To speak kindly does not hurt the tongue.

~ Proverb

REism

Profanity-laced tongue lashings are not Godly, regardless of the circumstance. It will leave a bad taste in your mouth. Avoid them at all cost! God would not approve.

RE
REAL EXCELLENCE

APRIL 21

The Best Weight Loss Program

Hebrews 12:1 ESV – Therefore, since we are surrounded by so great a cloud of witnesses, let us also lay aside every weight, and sin which clings so closely, and let us run with endurance the race that is set before us,

> A vigorous five-mile walk will do more good for an unhappy but otherwise healthy adult than all the medicine and psychology in the world.
>
> ~ Paul D. White

REism

Weightlifting can make you stronger, power walking can help you lose weight, but removing weights of sin from your body will give you the power of God.

RE

REAL EXCELLENCE

APRIL 22

I'm Better Today Than I Was Yesterday

Ephesians 5:15-17 ESV – Look carefully then how you walk, not as unwise but as wise, making the best use of the time, because the days are evil. Therefore do not be foolish, but understand what the will of the Lord is.

> Be open to learning new lessons even if they contradict the lessons you learned yesterday.
>
> ~ Ellen Degeneres

REism

Newfound information is what makes our today better than our yesterday.

OPEN-MINDEDNESS

RE
REAL EXCELLENCE

APRIL 23

Do The Math

Leviticus 7:23 ESV – Speak to the people of Israel, saying, You shall eat no fat, of ox or sheep or goat.

Every living cell in your body is made from the food you eat. If you consistently eat junk food then you'll have a junk body.

~ Jeanette Jenkins

REism

It's simple:

$$2 + 2 = 4$$
Junk Food = Junk Body!
Good Food = Good Body!

Eat Well!

APRIL 24

Shine Like The Sun

Hebrews 13:15 ESV – Through him then let us continually offer up a sacrifice of praise to God, that is, the fruit of lips that acknowledge his name.

> Turn your face to the sun and the shadows fall behind you.
>
> ~ Maori Proverb

REism

Let your attitude brighten even the cloudiest of days you encounter.

EXPRESSION OF POSITIVE ATTITUDE

RE

REAL EXCELLENCE

APRIL 25

Loving Your Wife

Ephesians 5:28 ESV – In the same way husbands should love their wives as their own bodies. He who loves his wife loves himself.

Always recognize that human individuals are ends, and do not use them as means to your end.

~ Immanuel Kant

REism

It is more than an emotional feeling or physical attraction. You must put her first! Men are to love their wives as Christ loved the church. What woman wouldn't respond to such a selfless display of love?

RELATIONSHIPS

APRIL 26

God's Oxygen

Job 27:3-4 ESV – as long as my breath is in me, and the spirit of God is in my nostrils, my lips will not speak falsehood, and my tongue will not utter deceit.

> You have to grow from the inside out. None can teach you, none can make you spiritual. There is no other teacher but your own soul.
>
> ~ Swami Vivekananda

REism

God's oxygen is the purest and most gratifying air we can breathe. It heals our soul and lifts up our spirit.

RE
REAL EXCELLENCE

APRIL 27

The Way to the Father

John 14:6 ESV – Jesus said to him, "I am the way, and the truth, and the life. No one comes to the Father except through me.

> Nothing can withstand the power of the human will if it is willing to stake its very existence to the extent of its purpose.
>
> ~ Benjamin Disraeli

REism

What is your life's purpose? Are you dedicated to your purpose? Are you willing to sacrifice your own existence?

APRIL 28

State of Mind

Psalm 119:16 ESV – I will delight in your statutes; I will not forget your word.

> The capacity to learn as a gift; The ability to learn is a skill; the willingness to learn is a choice.
>
> ~ Brian Herbert

REism

It all begins in your mind. What you give power to has power over you, if you allow it.

It's your choice!

EDUCATION

RE

REAL EXCELLENCE

APRIL 29

Loving Those Who Oppose You

Luke 6:32 ESV – If you love those who love you, what benefit is that to you? For even sinners love those who love them.

> The greater man the greater courtesy.
>
> ~ Alfred Lord Tennyson

REism

True strength and greatness is revealed when you show favor to your foes.

MANNERS

RE

REAL EXCELLENCE

APRIL 30

Hard Work Is Not For Sale

Proverbs 10:4 ESV – A slack hand causes poverty, but the hand of the diligent makes rich.

Physical fitness can neither be achieved by wishful thinking nor outright purchase.

~ Joseph Pilates

REism

Get off Fantasy Island, roll up your sleeves and WORK!

REAL EXCELLENCE

MAY

RE
REAL EXCELLENCE

MAY 1

Unlock the Secret

Jeremiah 33:3 ESV – Call to me and I will answer you, and will tell you great and hidden things that you have not known.

> I keep six honest serving-men,
> They taught me all I knew;
> Their names are What and Why and When
> And How and Where and Who.
>
> ~ Rudyard Kipling

REism

Keep your mind and heart open to God. You will notice that God has much to say!

RE

REAL EXCELLENCE

MAY 2

Grave Decisions

Leviticus 7:23-24 ESV – Speak to the people of Israel, saying, You shall eat no fat, of ox or sheep or goat. The fat of an animal that dies of itself and the fat of one that is torn by beasts may be put to any other use, but on no account shall you eat it.

Don't dig your grave with your own knife and fork.

~ English Proverb

REism

A well-balanced diet will help your body perform and recover quickly.

WELL-BALANCED NUTRITION

RE
REAL EXCELLENCE

MAY 3

Turning Negatives into Positives

John 15:27 ESV – And you also will bear witness, because you have been with me from the beginning.

> Oh, my friend, it's not what they take away from you that counts. It's what you do with what you have left.
>
> ~ Hubert Humphrey

REism

Your story is the key that can unlock someone else's prison. Share your testimony. God always leaves a lesson for us to learn after we come out of the storm. Take the lesson and help others who have the same struggles.

RE

REAL EXCELLENCE

MAY 4

Be Part of the Village

Proverbs 4:23 ESV – Keep your heart with all vigilance, for from it flow the springs of life.

> A neighborhood can raise a child, provide security, sustain our health, secure our income, and provide for vulnerable people. Each of these is within the power of our community.
>
> ~ John McKnight and Peter Block

REism

It is important to know the purpose for loving and helping others. It is your relationships with others by which you are remembered.

MAY 5

Appreciation Through Obedience

Acts 18:1-5 ESV – After this Paul left Athens and went to Corinth. And he found a Jew named Aquila, a native of Pontus, recently come from Italy with his wife Priscilla, because Claudius had commanded all the Jews to leave Rome. And he went to see them, and because he was of the same trade he stayed with them and worked, for they were tentmakers by trade. And he reasoned in the synagogue every Sabbath, and tried to persuade Jews and Greeks. When Silas and Timothy arrived from Macedonia, Paul was occupied with the word, testifying to the Jews that the Christ was Jesus.

Feeling grateful or appreciative of someone or something in your life actually attracts more of the things that you appreciate and value into your life.

~ Northrup Christiane

REism

Give thanks and praise to God always. He is the reason that you are blessed. Show your appreciation through your obedience.

MAY 6

Your Only Choice

Romans 4:20-25 ESV – No unbelief made him waver concerning the promise of God, but he grew strong in his faith as he gave glory to God, fully convinced that God was able to do what he had promised. That is why his faith was "counted to him as righteousness." But the words "it was counted to him" were not written for his sake alone, but for ours also. It will be counted to us who believe in him who raised from the dead Jesus our Lord, who was delivered up for our trespasses and raised for our justification.

> What this power is, I cannot say. All I know is that it exists...and it becomes available only when you are in that state of mind in which you know exactly what you want...and are fully determined not to quit until you get it.
>
> ~ Alexander Graham Bell

REism

You never know how strong you are until being strong is the only choice you have. God will always provide His children with a solution. Pay close attention to His Will and not your own.

DEDICATION

MAY 7

Your Drive into The Light

Proverbs 9:11 ESV – For by me your days will be multiplied, and years will be added to your life.

> Education is the movement from darkness to light.
>
> ~ Allan Bloom

REism

Education is the vehicle that can guide you toward great success.

MAY 8

Obeying Authorities

Titus 3:1-2 ESV – Remind them to be submissive to rulers and authorities, to be obedient, to be ready for every good work, to speak evil of no one, to avoid quarreling, to be gentle, and to show perfect courtesy toward all people.

Kind hearts are the gardens; kind thoughts are the roots; kind words are the blossoms; kind deeds are the fruits.

~ 19th century rhyme used in primary schools

REism

Obey those who have authority over you. This is right in the sight of the Lord. Knowing that the Lord has authority over all, let your actions speak louder than words.

MANNERS

MAY 9

Combining Youth and Wisdom

Proverbs 20:29 ESV – The glory of young men is their strength, but the splendor of old men is their gray hair.

> The adult were once young. The young have not yet attained adulthood. The young must learn to appreciate the wisdom of elderly people and learn from their life experiences.
>
> ~ Lailah Gifty Akita

REism

For God has called young men for their strength and old men for their wisdom to be one in Jesus Christ working together.

— PHYSICAL ACTIVITY —

RE

MAY 10

Be Open To Wise Counsel

Proverbs 15:22 ESV – Without counsel plans fail, but with many advisers they succeed.

Open your mind to the world and the many different ways that can be found in it, before making hasty judgments of others. After all, the very same thing that you judge from where you are— may very well be something totally different in meaning on the other side of the world.

~ C. JoyBell C.

REism

Keep your mind open to new things and different types of people. You never know who God is sending into your life to make it better.

OPEN-MINDEDNESS

MAY 11

The Importance of Nutritional Education

Philippians 3:19 ESV – Their end is destruction, their god is their belly, and they glory in their shame, with minds set on earthly things.

> Eating habits are learned behaviors; they're not intuitive.
>
> ~ Ann Cooper and Lisa M. Holmes

REism

Expanding your knowledge of food choices will enhance your ability to make healthier food choices. This is extremely important because the future of your life hangs in the balance.

WELL-BALANCED NUTRITION

MAY 12

Directing The Wind

Philippians 2:4 ESV – Let each of you look not only to his own interests, but also to the interests of others.

> We can't direct the wind, but we can adjust the sails. For maximum happiness, peace, and contentment, may we choose a positive attitude.
>
> ~ Thomas S. Monson

REism

A positive attitude is more than half the battle in a difficult situation. Adjust your sails and you may be able to direct the wind.

EXPRESSION OF POSITIVE ATTITUDE

MAY 13

A Piece Of The Puzzle

Psalm 85:10 ESV – Steadfast love and faithfulness meet; righteousness and peace kiss each other.

You are a piece of the puzzle of someone else's life. You may never know where you fit, but others will fill the holes in their lives with pieces of you.

~ Bonnie Arbor

REism

You may never know the importance of a relationship until it is no longer available. Enjoy and cherish the time you have with the people in your life and make memories that will last a lifetime.

MAY 14

Born Again

John 3:1-5 ESV – Now there was a man of the Pharisees named Nicodemus, a ruler of the Jews. This man came to Jesus by night and said to him, "Rabbi, we know that you are a teacher come from God, for no one can do these signs that you do unless God is with him." Jesus answered him, "Truly, truly, I say to you, unless one is born again he cannot see the kingdom of God." Nicodemus said to him, "How can a man be born when he is old? Can he enter a second time into his mother's womb and be born?" Jesus answered, "Truly, truly, I say to you, unless one is born of water and the Spirit, he cannot enter the kingdom of God.

If a man is to live, he must be all alive, body, soul, mind, heart, spirit.

~ Thomas Merto

REism

It is better to be born twice and die once, than to be born once and die twice. I promise you the second death you will not like.

ENRICHMENT OF SPIRIT

RE
REAL EXCELLENCE

MAY 15

Game On, Struggles

1 Samuel 1:11 ESV – And she vowed a vow and said, "O Lord of hosts, if you will indeed look on the affliction of your servant and remember me and not forget your servant, but will give to your servant a son, then I will give him to the Lord all the days of his life, and no razor shall touch his head."

> A life of total dedication to the truth also means a life of willingness to be personally challenged.
>
> ~ M. Scott Peck

REism

It takes an unwavering dedication throughout your journey to achieve your REal Excellence. You will not become dedicated by chance. Game on, struggles! I have God, so I can't lose, because God will never allow me to give up.

DEDICATION

RE

MAY 16

Your Light

Psalm 18:28 ESV – For it is you who light my lamp; the Lord my God lightens my darkness.

> The only person who is educated is the one who has learned how to learn and change.
>
> ~ Carl Rogers

REism

It is light that reveals Father God, and Jesus is the light of the world. In Him is life, and the life is the light of men.

Is your light on?

EDUCATION

MAY 17

Hospitality

Luke 7:44 ESV – Then turning toward the woman he said to Simon, "Do you see this woman? I entered your house; you gave me no water for my feet, but she has wet my feet with her tears and wiped them with her hair.

When you can be the sunshine in someone's life, or the warm rain, why would you be the cold north wind?

~ Robert Brault

REism

Showing good hospitality is using whatever you have to accommodate your guest. Love your neighbor and remember to be kind.

MANNERS

RE

MAY 18

Count Your Blessings and Be Honored

Psalm 144:1-15 ESV – Of David. Blessed be the Lord, my rock, who trains my hands for war, and my fingers for battle; he is my steadfast love and my fortress, my stronghold and my deliverer, my shield and he in whom I take refuge, who subdues peoples under me. O Lord, what is man that you regard him, or the son of man that you think of him? Man is like a breath; his days are like a passing shadow. Bow your heavens, O Lord, and come down! Touch the mountains so that they smoke!

If we could give every individual the right amount of nourishment and exercise, not too little and not too much, we would have found the safest way to health.

~ Hippocrates

REism

Taking care of your body should not be a chore, but an honor. There are many people who would love to trade their health for yours. Count your blessings, if you are physically able to exercise.

PHYSICAL ACTIVITY

MAY 19

Seek and Listen

Proverbs 19:20 ESV – Listen to advice and accept instruction, that you may gain wisdom in the future.

It takes a great man to be a good listener.

~ Calvin Coolidge

REism

Ask God to bless you with wisdom and discernment, and He will answer. Make sure you listen when He answers. The wisdom will equip you with the knowledge needed to make Godly decisions, and discernment will let you know when those decisions should be made.

OPEN-MINDEDNESS

MAY 20

Preventive Medicine

Ezekiel 4:9 ESV – And you, take wheat and barley, beans and lentils, millet and emmer, and put them into a single vessel and make your bread from them. During the number of days that you lie on your side, 390 days, you shall eat it.

> The doctor of the future will no longer treat the human frame with drugs, but rather will cure and prevent disease with nutrition.
>
> ~ Thomas Edison

REism

A well-balanced diet is the best preventive medicine for your body. Plan your meals, and good eating habits will form.

RE

REAL EXCELLENCE

MAY 21

Selfish Motives

Ezekiel 16:49-50 ESV – Behold, this was the guilt of your sister Sodom: she and her daughters had pride, excess of food, and prosperous ease, but did not aid the poor and needy. They were haughty and did an abomination before me. So I removed them, when I saw it.

> Almost every sinful action ever committed can be traced back to a selfish motive. It is a trait we hate in other people but justify in ourselves.
>
> ~ Stephen Kendrick, *The Love Dare*

REism

There really isn't any justification you can give! Selfish motives are not welcome into the gates of Heaven.

EXPRESSION OF POSITIVE ATTITUDE

RE
REAL EXCELLENCE

MAY 22

REal Friendship

Proverbs 17:17 ESV – A friend loves at all times, and a brother is born for adversity.

The world is so empty if one thinks only of mountains, rivers and cities; but to know someone who thinks and feels with us, and who, though distant, is close to us in spirit, this makes the earth for us an inhabited garden.

~ Johann Wolfgang von Goethe

REism

Friendships have been placed in our lives for a unique purpose and cause. Allow God to cultivate and sculpt your friendships.

RELATIONSHIPS

MAY 23

Fear and Faith

Romans 10:17 ESV – So faith comes from hearing, and hearing through the word of Christ.

Hope is faith holding out its hand in the dark.

~ George Iles

REism

Fear and faith have something in common. They both ask us to believe in something we cannot see. Faith can deliver us to a mountain top that fear would never attempt to climb.

RE

REAL EXCELLENCE

MAY 24

Quitting Is Not An Option

Leviticus 27:29 ESV – No one devoted, who is to be devoted for destruction from mankind, shall be ransomed; he shall surely be put to death.

> Struggle ends where commitment begins.
>
> ~ Sumner Davenport

REism

Nothing beats the passion you have in your heart and soul for your goal. Drive that passion even at the darkest of moments and stay committed to your goals. It is impossible to defeat a person who never quits!

DEDICATION

RE

REAL EXCELLENCE

MAY 25

Do You Know The Way?

Psalm 32:8-9 ESV – I will instruct you and teach you in the way you should go; I will counsel you with my eye upon you. Be not like a horse or a mule, without understanding, which must be curbed with bit and bridle, or it will not stay near you.

It is the mark of an educated mind to be able to entertain a thought without accepting it.

~ Aristotle

REism

The educated mind diligently seeks God's Word, and therefore is equipped with a Godly understanding. God will always show you the way He will have you go.

RE

REAL EXCELLENCE

MAY 26

Love and Joy

Matthew 7:12 ESV – So whatever you wish that others would do to you, do also to them, for this is the Law and the Prophets.

There is a courtesy of the heart; it is allied to love. From it springs the purest courtesy in the outward behavior.

~ Johann Wolfgang Von Goethe

REism

If you desire people to treat you in the most loving and joyous way, then love and joy must be your focus and how you interact with them. The heart that bleeds with love and joy is a peaceful heart and harms no one.

MANNERS

RE

REAL EXCELLENCE

MAY 27

Don't Let Appearances Fool You

1 Samuel 16:7 ESV – But the Lord said to Samuel, "Do not look on his appearance or on the height of his stature, because I have rejected him. For the Lord sees not as man sees: man looks on the outward appearance, but the Lord looks on the heart."

> Beauty that pleases the eye is a frail, fleeting illusion. But that beauty capable of pleasing the heart can endure endlessly.
>
> ~ Richelle E. Goodrich

REism

Since it is God who only knows what is in a person's heart, we must learn to discern what is coming from a person's heart. Outward appearances can be deceptive. The physically in-shape person could be the weakest person in the room.

PHYSICAL ACTIVITY

MAY 28

Installment Plan

Job 12:12-13 ESV – Wisdom is with the aged, and understanding in length of days. "With God are wisdom and might; he has counsel and understanding.

> There is a plan to this universe. There is a high intelligence, maybe even a purpose, but it's given to us on the installment plan.
>
> ~ Isaac Bashevis Singer

REism

God has a plan for each of us, and His blessings are plentiful. Ask Him to reveal a piece of His plan for your life each day. Make sure you savor all blessings and add them to your installment plan.

OPEN-MINDEDNESS

MAY 29

Just and Unjust Intake

Ephesians 5:18 ESV – And do not get drunk with wine, for that is debauchery, but be filled with the Spirit.

With the wrong diet, no medicine can help.
With the right diet, no medicine is necessary.

~ Ayurvedic Proverb

REism

The inspired word of God is Spirit and truth. Seek to be filled with God's Spiritual food. Watch very closely what you take into your mouth and mind. Your body responds accordingly to every just and unjust intake.

WELL-BALANCED NUTRITION

MAY 30

Wiping The Slate Clean

1 John 1:9 ESV – If we confess our sins, he is faithful and just to forgive us our sins and to cleanse us from all unrighteousness.

Dwell not upon thy weariness, thy strength shall be according to the measure of thy desire.

~ Arab Proverb

REism

Open your heart and pray. Ask God to forgive you for your shortcomings and move forward with faith that God will forgive you. Then pray for God to give you the necessary tools to stay strong in your walk with Christ.

EXPRESSION OF POSITIVE ATTITUDE

RE
REAL EXCELLENCE

MAY 31

You Make Me Whole

1 Corinthians 7:9 ESV – But if they cannot exercise self-control, they should marry. For it is better to marry than to burn with passion.

> When we seek for connection, we restore the world to wholeness. Our seemingly separate lives become meaningful as we discover how truly necessary we are to each other.
>
> ~ Margaret Wheatley

REism

When you say, "I do" and commit to living an interdependent life with your spouse, you become whole!

RELATIONSHIPS

JUNE

RE
REAL EXCELLENCE

JUNE 1

The Transformation of Hope

Colossians 1:1-5 ESV – Paul, an apostle of Christ Jesus by the will of God, and Timothy our brother, To the saints and faithful brothers in Christ at Colossae: Grace to you and peace from God our Father. We always thank God, the Father of our Lord Jesus Christ, when we pray for you, since we heard of your faith in Christ Jesus and of the love that you have for all the saints, because of the hope laid up for you in heaven. Of this you have heard before in the word of the truth, the gospel,

> Hope transforms pessimism into optimism. Hope is invincible. Hope changes everything. It changes winter into summer, darkness into dawn, descent into ascent, barrenness into creativity, agony into joy. Hope is the sun. It is light. It is passion. It is the fundamental force for life's blossoming.
>
> ~ Daisaku Ike

REism

Give thanks to God for strengthening our hope and turning it into faith.

ENRICHMENT OF SPIRIT

RE

REAL EXCELLENCE

JUNE 2

That's My Favorite Song!
Can You Rewind or Pause It?

Psalm 150:1-5 ESV – Praise the Lord! Praise God in his sanctuary; praise him in his mighty heavens! Praise him for his mighty deeds; praise him according to his excellent greatness! Praise him with trumpet sound; praise him with lute and harp! Praise him with tambourine and dance; praise him with strings and pipe! Praise him with sounding cymbals; praise him with loud clashing cymbals!

> Keep your dreams alive. Understand to achieve anything requires faith and belief in yourself, vision, hard work, determination, and dedication. Remember all things are possible for those who believe.
>
> ~ Gail Devers

REism

We all have that favorite song that we rewind and replay over and over, or pause whenever we are interrupted while listening to it. Life would be perfect if failure had fast forward buttons and good times had pause buttons. That is not the case, but we do have dedication and determination!

──────────── **DEDICATION** ────────────

JUNE 3

The Author and Finisher

2 Peter 1:5 ESV – For this very reason, make every effort to supplement your faith with virtue, and virtue with knowledge,

---

Live as if you were to die tomorrow. Learn as if you were to live forever.

~ Mahatma Gandhi

REism

Morally live your life by applying the teachings of God's Word. Seek the knowledge of God's Kingdom and allow Jesus to be the author and finisher of your faith.

RE
REAL EXCELLENCE

JUNE 4

Love For All and All For The Love Of God

1 John 4:19 ESV – We love because he first loved us.

> The first point of courtesy must always be love!
>
> ~ Ralph Waldo Emerson

REism

We love now because even when we were an enemy of God, He still loved for us first. Find an enemy and love on them!

Love generously and show love to everyone you know!

JUNE 5

Mentally Connected

2 Peter 1:5-7 ESV – For this very reason, make every effort to supplement your faith with virtue, and virtue with knowledge, and knowledge with self-control, and self-control with steadfastness, and steadfastness with godliness, and godliness with brotherly affection, and brotherly affection with love.

True enjoyment comes from activity of the mind and exercise of the body; the two are ever united.

~ Wilhelm von Humboldt

REism

Mind, Body and Soul are vital to your success. Are you struggling to mentally connect with your workout?

Call upon the Holy Spirit to help you with your challenges.

PHYSICAL ACTIVITY

JUNE 6

Sometimes Silence is Best

Proverbs 17:27-28 ESV – Whoever restrains his words has knowledge, and he who has a cool spirit is a man of understanding. Even a fool who keeps silent is considered wise; when he closes his lips, he is deemed intelligent.

It is better to remain silent at the risk of being thought a fool, than to talk and remove all doubt of it. ~ Maurice Switzer

REism

You always best serve yourself with silence when you lack knowledge or facts about a situation.

OPEN-MINDEDNESS

JUNE 7

The Bearing Of Fruit

John 12:24 ESV – Truly, truly, I say to you, unless a grain of wheat falls into the earth and dies, it remains alone; but if it dies, it bears much fruit.

No single food will make or break good health. But the kinds of food you choose day in and day out have a major impact.

~ Walter Willet

REism

Not until something dies can it be planted and produce much fruit. The Christian walk requires us to plant our life with Jesus Christ in the likeness of His death. We shall seek to be like Him in the resurrection.

WELL-BALANCED NUTRITION

RE

JUNE 8

Contagious

John 8:31-32 ESV – So Jesus said to the Jews who had believed him, "If you abide in my word, you are truly my disciples, and you will know the truth, and the truth will set you free.

Attitudes are contagious. Are yours worth catching?

~ Dennis and Wendy Mannering

REism

Understand the importance of following Christ. You are a walking testimony! Be sure to set an example that is contagious and speaks the truth about God.

EXPRESSION OF POSITIVE ATTITUDE

JUNE 9

Every Single Person Matters

Luke 6:31 ESV – And as you wish that others would do to you, do so to them.

> We are all a part of every person we have ever met.
>
> ~ Alfred Lord Tennyson

REism

It is simple: Treat everyone you meet the way you would want to be treated!

RE
REAL EXCELLENCE

JUNE 10

The Storms of Life

2 Corinthians 4:8-9 ESV – We are afflicted in every way, but not crushed; perplexed, but not driven to despair; persecuted, but not forsaken; struck down, but not destroyed;

> Clouds or no clouds, life is grand — be grateful for all the varieties of weather in your life.
>
> ~ Terri Guillemets

REism

Whether you are in a storm, coming out of a storm or approaching a storm, God is there too, and through prayer and faith He will provide shelter. Trusting in God will give you the strength needed to dance in the rain!

JUNE 11

Keep Grinding

Ezra 6:16 ESV – And the people of Israel, the priests and the Levites, and the rest of the returned exiles, celebrated the dedication of this house of God with joy.

> Sometimes it's necessary to go a long distance out of the way in order to come back a short distance correctly.
>
> ~ Edward Albee

REism

Sometimes we must take a step back to reach our Godly destination. Stay on the grind!

DEDICATION

RE

REAL EXCELLENCE

JUNE 12

Leading The Horse to Water

Luke 13:33 ESV – Nevertheless, I must go on my way today and tomorrow and the day following, for it cannot be that a prophet should perish away from Jerusalem.

> Teachers open the door, but you must enter by yourself.
>
> ~ Chinese Proverb

REism

Wisdom is the substance that knowledge does not comprehend. Pray for God to grant you wisdom, because it is your wisdom that will quench your thirst with the drinking water approved by God.

EDUCATION

JUNE 13

Controlling The Tongue

Proverbs 21:23 ESV – Whoever keeps his mouth and his tongue keeps himself out of trouble.

Silence is not always tact and it is tact that is golden, not silence.

~ Samuel Butler

REism

Learn to bridle your tongue and you will avoid much trouble. But only through the Holy Spirit can one control their tongue.

RE
REAL EXCELLENCE

JUNE 14

Lifting Up Your Hands

Hebrews 12:12 ESV – Therefore lift your drooping hands and strengthen your weak knees,

---

Health is the thing that makes you feel that now is the best time of the year.

~ Franklin Pierce Adams

REism

If we lift up our hands unto Jesus in total submission, He will strengthen our knees to move onward and upward. It is the best lifting exercise you can do.

PHYSICAL ACTIVITY

JUNE 15

Can You Hear God?

Colossians 3:16 ESV – Let the word of Christ dwell in you richly, teaching and admonishing one another in all wisdom, singing psalms and hymns and spiritual songs, with thankfulness in your hearts to God.

> We have eyelids but not ear lids, for the ears are the portals of learning, and Nature wanted to keep them wide open.
>
> ~ Baltasar Gracián

REism

God whispers in our joy, but He shouts in our pain! He is making sure we hear Him! Faith is obtained by hearing the words of God through the scriptures of the Bible.

Is God trying to get your attention?

OPEN-MINDEDNESS

RE

JUNE 16

You Are Invited To The Feast

Isaiah 25:6 ESV – On this mountain the Lord of hosts will make for all peoples a feast of rich food, a feast of well-aged wine, of rich food full of marrow, of aged wine well refined.

> Tell me what you eat, and I will tell you who you are.
>
> ~ Jean Anthelme Brillat-Savarin

REism

The Lord desires your presence at His feast on Mount Zion. Eat God's Word and make it to the feast.

WELL-BALANCED NUTRITION

RE

REAL EXCELLENCE

JUNE 17

Are You a Pessimist or an Optimist?

Hebrews 11:1 ESV – Now faith is the assurance of things hoped for, the conviction of things not seen.

> A pessimist sees the difficulty in every opportunity; an optimist sees the opportunity in every difficulty.
>
> ~ Winston Churchill

REism

Faith is Spiritual optimism. It is difficult to shake in the midst of a storm. It also holds true in lightness and in darkness. Learn to think Spiritually.

EXPRESSION OF POSITIVE ATTITUDE

JUNE 18

Paving The Way

Isaiah 43:10 ESV – "You are my witnesses," declares the Lord, "and my servant whom I have chosen, that you may know and believe me and understand that I am he. Before me no god was formed, nor shall there be any after me.

> Be the change you want to see in the world.
>
> ~ Mahatma Gandhi

REism

God sent you to pave the path of greatness for the next generation. Therefore your relationship with God is paramount to paving the path of righteousness.

RELATIONSHIPS

RE

REAL EXCELLENCE

JUNE 19

The Love of Money and Material Things

Hebrews 13:5 ESV – Keep your life free from love of money, and be content with what you have, for he has said, "I will never leave you nor forsake you."

Let's be cautious about relying so much on material things that we have no energy left for the spiritual aspects of our lives.

~ James A. Forbes

REism

Never be so busy and concerned about earning a living that you neglect to live a life honoring God. Ways to honor God: Love God first and with all your heart; Use money in ways that will glorify God; Give Graciously; Thank God for His Blessings; Be Grateful for what God has entrusted you with; Forgive others and Pray for all!

ENRICHMENT OF SPIRIT

RE
REAL EXCELLENCE

JUNE 20

Dream Big

1 Samuel 1:27-28 ESV – For this child I prayed, and the Lord has granted me my petition that I made to him. Therefore I have lent him to the Lord. As long as he lives, he is lent to the Lord." And he worshiped the Lord there.

> The future belongs to those who believe in the beauty of their dreams.
>
> ~ Eleanor Roosevelt

REism

Dream so big that you have to grow into the person who has to achieve them, and believe that God will breathe life into the dreams you have envisioned. Believing in your dreams will keep you dedicated to your dreams!

— DEDICATION —

RE
REAL EXCELLENCE

JUNE 21

The Value of the Heart

Psalm 119:99 ESV – I have more understanding than all my teachers, for your testimonies are my meditation.

Children must be taught how to think, not what to think.

~ Margaret Mead

REism

Don't educate your children to be monetarily rich. Educate them to have a joyfully rich heart, so they learn the value of the heart and not the value of the price.

RE

REAL EXCELLENCE

JUNE 22

Life is Shorter Than You Think

Ephesians 4:32 ESV – Be kind to one another, tenderhearted, forgiving one another, as God in Christ forgave you.

> You cannot do a kindness too soon, for you never know how soon it will be too late.
>
> ~ Ralph Waldo Emerson

REism

Kindness begins in the heart and grows into a bouquet of compassion! Call someone you haven't talked to in a while and tell them how much you miss them.

MANNERS

RE
REAL EXCELLENCE

JUNE 23

Are You Willing to Work For Food?

2 Thessalonians 3:10 ESV – For even when we were with you, we would give you this command: If anyone is not willing to work, let him not eat.

> Thinking about working out burns 0 calories,
> 0 percentage of fat and accomplishes 0 goals!
>
> ~ Gwen Ro

REism

In order to have daily provisions one must work. God calls us to do good work that relates to His business. Let's work while we can for our Father's business.

PHYSICAL ACTIVITY

RE
REAL EXCELLENCE

JUNE 24

From The Hear To The Heart

Revelation 2:7 – He who has an ear, let him hear what the Spirit says to the churches. To the one who conquers I will grant to eat of the tree of life, which is in the paradise of God.

> Flexibility requires an open mind and a welcoming of new alternatives.
>
> ~ Deborah Day

REism

Blessed is the one who seeks to position himself or herself to hear the word of God and hide God's Word in their heart.

Position yourself!

JUNE 25

You Will Be Rewarded

Colossians 3:23-24 ESV – Whatever you do, work heartily, as for the Lord and not for men, knowing that from the Lord you will receive the inheritance as your reward. You are serving the Lord Christ.

> Just like your body and lifestyle can be healthy or unhealthy, the same is true with your beliefs. Your beliefs can be your medicine or your poison.
>
> ~ Steve Maraboli

REism

Train your mind to REward your body with healthy choices. Just as Christ blesses His children, your body will be REwarded for your healthy eating choices. Your body can't produce good fruit from bad seeds.

WELL-BALANCED NUTRITION

RE
REAL EXCELLENCE

JUNE 26

Joy: A State of Being

Job 10:15 ESV – If I am guilty, woe to me! If I am in the right, I cannot lift up my head, for I am filled with disgrace and look on my affliction.

> Happiness depends less on what happens to us and more on how we view the past positively, enjoy the moment and create the future.
>
> ~ Shannon L. Alder

REism

A joyful heart is the best medicine for everyday living. Joy doesn't require an action or circumstance because it is a state of being. It exists no matter what kind of day we are having. Choose a joyful spirit and watch it have a positive effect on your future.

EXPRESSION OF POSITIVE ATTITUDE

RE

REAL EXCELLENCE

JUNE 27

Fellowship Group

2 Corinthians 6:11-13 ESV – We have spoken freely to you, Corinthians; our heart is wide open. You are not restricted by us, but you are restricted in your own affections. In return (I speak as to children) widen your hearts also.

> No man is an island, entire of itself; every man is a piece of the continent, a part of the main.
>
> ~ John Donne

REism

Fellowship with each other as God commands. There is potential to grow from being connected to a group of believers and followers of Christ.

If you haven't done so already, join a fellowship group today!

RELATIONSHIPS

JUNE 28

Cheerful Heart

Colossians 3:17 ESV – And whatever you do, in word or deed, do everything in the name of the Lord Jesus, giving thanks to God the Father through him.

> The heart that truly loves never forgets.
>
> ~ Proverb

REism

Do not do things with a begrudging heart. Have a cheerful spirit in everything you do.

RE

REAL EXCELLENCE

JUNE 29

He's Waiting On You

Hebrews 10:26 ESV – For if we go on sinning deliberately after receiving the knowledge of the truth, there no longer remains a sacrifice for sins,

---

> Often, it's not about becoming a new person, but becoming the person you were meant to be, and already are, but don't know how to be.
>
> ~ Heath L. Buckmaster

REism

Ask God to help you become the person He intended you to become. After all, we are what God thinks we are.

Make sure you are ready for the answer!

RE
REAL EXCELLENCE

JUNE 30

The Heart and Soul of Our House

Deuteronomy 6:6-9 ESV – And these words that I command you today shall be on your heart. You shall teach them diligently to your children, and shall talk of them when you sit in your house, and when you walk by the way, and when you lie down, and when you rise. You shall bind them as a sign on your hand, and they shall be as frontlets between your eyes. You shall write them on the doorposts of your house and on your gates.

Educating the mind without educating the heart is no education at all.

~ Aristotle

REism

First we must have the word of God in our heart. This will allow us to teach our children the word of God. We must do this with due diligence at all times presenting to them Jesus, who is our Lord and Savior. Seeing Christ Jesus being lived out in our lives will REsonate in their heart.

EDUCATION

JULY

JULY 1

Loving Your Enemy

Luke 6:35 ESV – But love your enemies, and do good, and lend, expecting nothing in return, and your reward will be great, and you will be sons of the Most High, for he is kind to the ungrateful and the evil.

> How beautiful a day can be when kindness touches it!
>
> ~ George Elliston

REism

Forgive people in your life, even those who are not sorry for their actions. Holding on to anger only hurts you, not them.

MANNERS

RE
REAL EXCELLENCE

JULY 2

Your Daily Prayer Workout

James 5:16 ESV – Therefore, confess your sins to one another and pray for one another, that you may be healed. The prayer of a righteous person has great power as it is working.

> Our love to God is measured by our everyday fellowship with others and how it's displayed.
>
> ~ Andrew Murray

REism

Are you looking for an amazing workout? Here's one! Make a habit of going to God in prayer for your fellow Christians daily.

RE

REAL EXCELLENCE

JULY 3

The Breakthrough is Coming

Colossians 2:1-3 ESV – For I want you to know how great a struggle I have for you and for those at Laodicea and for all who have not seen me face to face, that their hearts may be encouraged, being knit together in love, to reach all the riches of full assurance of understanding and the knowledge of God's mystery, which is Christ, in whom are hidden all the treasures of wisdom and knowledge.

> By seeking and blundering we learn.
>
> ~ Johann Wolfgang von Goethe

REism

Sometimes it takes an overwhelming breakdown to have an undeniable breakthrough.

JULY 4

Equipped With The Basic Fundamentals

2 Timothy 3:16-17 ESV – All Scripture is breathed out by God and profitable for teaching, for reproof, for correction, and for training in righteousness, that the man of God may be complete, equipped for every good work.

> Proper nutrition is one of the most fundamental things on which anyone's healthy and happy life can be based.
>
> ~ Sahara Sanders

REism

Are you covering the basics?
- Vegetables and fruits
- Grain (cereal) foods, mostly wholegrain and/or high fiber varieties
- Lean meats and poultry, fish, eggs, tofu, nuts, seeds and legumes/beans
- Milk, yogurt cheese and/or alternatives, mostly reduced fat

WELL-BALANCED NUTRITION

JULY 5

Choose Faith

Proverbs 17:22 ESV – A joyful heart is good medicine, but a crushed spirit dries up the bones.

> A happy person is not a person in a certain set of circumstances, but rather a person with a certain set of attitudes.
>
> ~ Hugh Downs

REism

Your Faith can move mountains, and your doubt can create them.

Affirmation: I choose Faith!

RE

JULY 6

Good Morning, My Love

1 Peter 4:8-10 ESV – Above all, keep loving one another earnestly, since love covers a multitude of sins. Show hospitality to one another without grumbling. As each has received a gift, use it to serve one another, as good stewards of God's varied grace:

> A good morning text doesn't only mean "good morning". It has a silent loving message that says... "I think of you when I wake up."
>
> ~ Unknown

REism

Be with someone who will take very good care of you, not just materialistically, but one who will also take notice of the simplest of things that mean so much, like "Good Morning, My Love!"

Never let the sun rise and you not say "Good Morning!"

RELATIONSHIPS

RE
REAL EXCELLENCE

JULY 7

The Next Minute Is Not Promised

Psalm 136:1 ESV – Give thanks to the Lord, for he is good, for his steadfast love endures forever.

It is through gratitude for the present moment that the spiritual dimension of life opens up.

~ Eckhart Tolle

REism

Life is an amazing journey. One day, one hour, and one minute will never come again in your entire life. Let go of anger and love one another as God loved the church. Our next minute is not promised.

JULY 8

Giving Your Best

2 Timothy 2:15 ESV – Do your best to present yourself to God as one approved, a worker who has no need to be ashamed, rightly handling the word of truth.

> We have to do the best we can. This is our sacred human responsibility.
>
> ~ Albert Einstein

REism

God knows best, so giving your best effort will always be pleasing to God.

Have you been giving your best?

DEDICATION

RE

REAL EXCELLENCE

JULY 9

Your Personal Measuring Stick

Isaiah 46:8 ESV – Remember this and stand firm, recall it to mind, you transgressors,

---

> Spoon feeding in the long run teaches us nothing but the shape of the spoon.
>
> ~ E.M. Forster

REism

Test your knowledge and keep accurate records of the REsults. It will REveal your progress!

RE

REAL EXCELLENCE

JULY 10

You're Not The Problem

Proverbs 11:17 ESV – A man who is kind benefits himself, but a cruel man hurts himself.

> No one is more insufferable than he who lacks basic courtesy.
>
> ~ Robert Brault

REism

If someone treats you badly, just remember that there is something wrong with them, not you. Godly people don't go around destroying other human beings.

MANNERS

RE

REAL EXCELLENCE

JULY 11

Do You!

Luke 1:1 ESV – Inasmuch as many have undertaken to compile a narrative of the things that have been accomplished among us,

---

> Getting fit is all about mind over matter. I don't mind, so it doesn't matter.
>
> ~ Adam Hargreaves

REism

Physical fitness is not about being better than someone else, it's about being the best you.

RE

REAL EXCELLENCE

JULY 12

Are You Really Listening?

Proverbs 18:13 ESV – If one gives an answer before he hears, it is his folly and shame.

> Most people do not listen with the intent to understand; they listen with the intent to reply.
>
> ~ Stephen R. Covey

REism

Try this, it works! Listen first. Think second. React slowly and be in tune to what was said.

RE

REAL EXCELLENCE

JULY 13

All Of You

Deuteronomy 6:4-5 ESV – Hear, O Israel: The Lord our God, the Lord is one. You shall love the Lord your God with all your heart and with all your soul and with all your might.

> It's up to you today to start making healthy choices.
>
> ~ Steve Maraboli

REism

It is my will to obey God by using every fiber of my body, including my choices in food and desires of my heart. All this is so I might know His joy.

WELL-BALANCED NUTRITION

JULY 14

Believers and Doubters

James 1:6 ESV – But let him ask in faith, with no doubting, for the one who doubts is like a wave of the sea that is driven and tossed by the wind.

One of the greatest discoveries a person makes, one of his great surprises, is to fine that they can do with they were afraid that they could not do.

~ Henry Ford

REism

Sometimes you have to stop worrying, thinking and doubting. Be a believer and have faith that things will work out as God sees fit.

JULY 15

Just One

Psalm 82:3-4 ESV – Give justice to the weak and the fatherless; maintain the right of the afflicted and the destitute. Rescue the weak and the needy; deliver them from the hand of the wicked.

> Help the life of one person and you can help the community.
>
> ~ Steven Sawalich

REism

Continue doing God's earthly work, and even if your life's work only delivers one person to God, it will increase God's Kingdom. Well done, my faithful servant!

RE
REAL EXCELLENCE

JULY 16

Inner Spirit

Ephesians 1:16 ESV – I do not cease to give thanks for you, remembering you in my prayers,

---

We can travel great distances in search of beauty and we can open our eyes to the simple pleasure that surrounds us every day, breathe in, and appreciate their wonders.

~ Lisa Desatnik

REism

Close your eyes and allow your mind to travel to the most beautiful place on Earth. Breathe and exhale slowly; you will feel a calm come over your body. Thank God for blessing us with our inner spirit.

ENRICHMENT OF SPIRIT

RE
REAL EXCELLENCE

JULY 17

Connected To The Vine Of REal Excellence

1 Chronicles 29:16-18 ESV – O Lord our God, all this abundance that we have provided for building you a house for your holy name comes from your hand and is all your own. I know, my God, that you test the heart and have pleasure in uprightness. In the uprightness of my heart I have freely offered all these things, and now I have seen your people, who are present here, offering freely and joyously to you. O Lord, the God of Abraham, Isaac, and Israel, our fathers, keep forever such purposes and thoughts in the hearts of your people, and direct their hearts toward you.

> Those who attain any excellence commonly spend life in one pursuit; for excellence is not often granted upon easier terms.
>
> ~ Samuel Johnson

REism

The vine of all REal Excellence starts with the heart and travels through the process with fortitude. We must make it our will to love God with all of our heart, with all of our soul, with all of our being. To love is to obey and he who obeys the gospel is connected to the vine of REal Excellence.

—————— **DEDICATION** ——————

JULY 18

Payday is Coming

Jeremiah 17:10 ESV – I the Lord search the heart and test the mind, to give every man according to his ways, according to the fruit of his deeds.

> Education is our passport to the future, for tomorrow belongs to the people who prepare for it today.
>
> ~ Malcolm X

REism

If you plant good seeds, a good tree will grow and bring forth good fruit. A well planted seed today will pay positive dividends tomorrow.

RE

REAL EXCELLENCE

JULY 19

A Simple Hello Goes A Long Way

Colossians 3:12 ESV – Put on then, as God's chosen ones, holy and beloved, compassionate hearts, kindness, humility, meekness, and patience,

---

If today you can't be anything else to anybody, you can be the passing stranger who nodded hello.

~ Robert Brault

REism

Saying hello adds warmth and comfort, even for a stranger.

MANNERS

RE

REAL EXCELLENCE

JULY 20

REal Excellence Requires Commitment

Hebrews 6:12 ESV – So that you may not be sluggish, but imitators of those who through faith and patience inherit the promises.

> A lack of exercise robs the body of an essential ingredient.
>
> ~ Karen Sessions

REism

Commitment is unconditional, and there is no expiration date!

LET'S GO!

RE
REAL EXCELLENCE

JULY 21

Ask and You Shall Receive

James 1:5 ESV – If any of you lacks wisdom, let him ask God, who gives generously to all without reproach, and it will be given him.

> If we are open only to discoveries which will accord with what we know already, we may as well stay shut.
>
> ~ Alan Watts

REism

The Bible says, "Ask and you shall receive." Is it really that simple? Yes, because asking a question can open your mind to an another answer different to what you were thinking. That is how we grow and learn!

JULY 22

Virtual Tour

2 Peter 1:5 ESV – For this very reason, make every effort to supplement your faith with virtue, and virtue with knowledge,

---

Healthy habits harbor happiness.

~ Zero Dean

REism

Knowing what God has in store for those who love Him allows us to take the virtual walk on Earth in a highly moral, spiritually fed body.

JULY 23

Change Starts in The Mind

Deuteronomy 31:6 ESV – Be strong and courageous. Do not fear or be in dread of them, for it is the Lord your God who goes with you. He will not leave you or forsake you.

> Change your thoughts and you change your world.
>
> ~ Norman Vincent Peal

REism

Are you facing change and struggling with the unknown? Take it to God, meditate on His word and trust His answers. God will not forsake you!

EXPRESSION OF POSITIVE ATTITUDE

JULY 24

I Forgive You

Romans 15:5 ESV – May the God of endurance and encouragement grant you to live in such harmony with one another, in accord with Christ Jesus,

> The most important single ingredient in the formula of success is knowing how to get along with people.
>
> ~ Theodore Roosevelt

REism

All relationships will experience some form of hardship and dissatisfaction. The REal testament of a relationship can be found in one's ability to forgive.

RELATIONSHIPS

JULY 25

Impossible to Man, But Possible With God

Hebrews 13:15 ESV – Through him then let us continually offer up a sacrifice of praise to God, that is, the fruit of lips that acknowledge his name.

> We need as many ways as possible to live the spirit of spirituality.
>
> ~ Anne Wilson Schaef

REism

Feed your faith with God's Word continuously, and your fears will starve to death. This type of spiritual feeding is a breastplate for making what might appear impossible to man, but possible with God.

RE

REAL EXCELLENCE

JULY 26

Knowing Your Weaknesses

1 Peter 5:8-11 ESV – Be sober-minded; be watchful. Your adversary the devil prowls around like a roaring lion, seeking someone to devour. Resist him, firm in your faith, knowing that the same kinds of suffering are being experienced by your brotherhood throughout the world. And after you have suffered a little while, the God of all grace, who has called you to his eternal glory in Christ, will himself restore, confirm, strengthen, and establish you. To him be the dominion forever and ever. Amen.

Accept yourself, your strengths, your weaknesses, your truths, and know what tools you have to fulfill your purpose.

~ Steve Maraboli,
Life, the Truth, and Being Free

REism

I am strong because I know my weaknesses. Dedicate your life to realizing and resisting temptation. Take all known weaknesses to God in prayer daily.

—————————— **DEDICATION** ——————————

JULY 27

The Hidden Treasures of Life

Amos 3:7 ESV – For the Lord God does nothing without revealing his secret to his servants the prophets.

> The locked door in my house is just a diversion. The real valuable items are out in the open, where they are hidden from the unimaginative..
>
> ~ Jarod Kintz

REism

The key to life's hidden treasures can be found in the books and material you refuse to read.

RE

REAL EXCELLENCE

JULY 28

Your Testimony

Proverbs 31:26 ESV – She opens her mouth with wisdom, and the teaching of kindness is on her tongue.

> A generous heart, kind speech, & a life of service & compassion are the things which renew humanity.
>
> ~ Buddha

REism

Look for opportunities to share your testimony. You never know when your story may bring someone else to Christ.

Reach out and share your testimony with someone today.

MANNERS

RE

REAL EXCELLENCE

JULY 29

Exercising The Heart

Colossians 3:23 ESV – Whatever you do, work heartily, as for the Lord and not for men,

---

Let us practice the fine art of making every work a priestly ministration. Let us believe that God is in all our simple deeds and learn to find Him there.

~ A.W. Tozer

REism

In all the work you do today, keep your focus on pleasing God. A well-exercised heart is pleasing to God. A great exercise for the Heart is being a blessing to someone else.

What heart exercises have you done today?

PHYSICAL ACTIVITY

RE
REAL EXCELLENCE

JULY 30

You Can't Always Be Right

Proverbs 3:13-17 ESV – Blessed is the one who finds wisdom, and the one who gets understanding, for the gain from her is better than gain from silver and her profit better than gold. She is more precious than jewels, and nothing you desire can compare with her. Long life is in her right hand; in her left hand are riches and honor. Her ways are ways of pleasantness, and all her paths are peace.

> A person with a fixed idea will always find some way of convincing himself in the end that he is right.
>
> ~ Atle Selberg

REism

Thinking you are always right will lead to your demise. Acknowledging your wrongs can send one in search of what's right! To live a creative life, we must lose our fear of being wrong.

Being Wrong Can Be Better Than Believing You Are Always Right!

OPEN-MINDEDNESS

RE

REAL EXCELLENCE

JULY 31

Fasting In Prayer

Acts 27:33-34 ESV – As day was about to dawn, Paul urged them all to take some food, saying, "Today is the fourteenth day that you have continued in suspense and without food, having taken nothing. Therefore I urge you to take some food. For it will give you strength, for not a hair is to perish from the head of any of you."

> A fast is not necessarily something we offer God, but it assists us in offering ourselves.
>
> ~ Jen Hatmaker

REism

Fasting is an opportunity to deeply connect with your prayers and offer your bodily hunger as a sacrifice.

WELL-BALANCED NUTRITION

AUGUST

RE
REAL EXCELLENCE

AUGUST 1

Imitating Christ

1 Corinthians 11:1-5 ESV – Be imitators of me, as I am of Christ. Now I commend you because you remember me in everything and maintain the traditions even as I delivered them to you. But I want you to understand that the head of every man is Christ, the head of a wife is her husband, and the head of Christ is God. Every man who prays or prophesies with his head covered dishonors his head, but every wife who prays or prophesies with her head uncovered dishonors her head, since it is the same as if her head were shaven.

> Very often a change of self is needed more than a change of scene.
>
> ~ Arthur Christopher Benson

REism

Does your life imitate Christ, or does it imitate the world? Change is good, but changing for Christ is divine.

EXPRESSION OF POSITIVE ATTITUDE

RE

REAL EXCELLENCE

AUGUST 2

Takers and Givers

Philippians 2:3 ESV – Do nothing from rivalry or conceit, but in humility count others more significant than yourselves.

> We make a living by what we get; we make a life by what we give.
>
> ~ Winston Churchill

REism

There are two types of people: takers and givers. Takers are selfish in conceit; givers are selfless in humility.

Which one are you?

AUGUST 3

Your Lighthouse

Hebrews 12:28 ESV – Therefore let us be grateful for receiving a kingdom that cannot be shaken, and thus let us offer to God acceptable worship, with reverence and awe,

> A living faith will last in the midst of the blackest storm.
>
> ~ Mahatma Gandhi

REism

Lead life with Christ as your lighthouse. It is the only way to make it back to God safely.

RE

REAL EXCELLENCE

AUGUST 4

Brush Your Shoulders Off

Proverbs 22:1-5 ESV – A good name is to be chosen rather than great riches, and favor is better than silver or gold. The rich and the poor meet together; the Lord is the maker of them all. The prudent sees danger and hides himself, but the simple go on and suffer for it. The reward for humility and fear of the Lord is riches and honor and life. Thorns and snares are in the way of the crooked; whoever guards his soul will keep far from them.

You will face your greatest opposition when you are closest to your biggest miracle.

~ Shannon L. Alder

REism

Don't be shocked to find out that your greatest opposition is the haters.

Here's how the conversation should go with a hater—The hater will say, "I think your dream is too big."

You should say, "That's only because you think too small!"

DEDICATION

227

RE

REAL EXCELLENCE

AUGUST 5

Seek Knowledge At All Cost

Proverbs 8:10 ESV – Take my instruction instead of silver, and knowledge rather than choice gold,

> Learning is not attained by chance, it must be sought for with ardor and attended to with diligence.
>
> ~ Abigail Adams

REism

Godly instructions and knowledge of God's Word are better than any monetary gain.

RE

REAL EXCELLENCE

AUGUST 6

The Unknown to You

Isaiah 55:11 ESV – so shall my word be that goes out from my mouth; it shall not return to me empty, but it shall accomplish that which I purpose, and shall succeed in the thing for which I sent it.

> Be kind, for everyone you meet is fighting a harder battle.
>
> ~ Plato

REism

You never know what someone else is dealing with. That is why it is always best to lead with kindness.

AUGUST 7

Priority

Revelation 1:8 ESV – "I am the Alpha and the Omega," says the Lord God, "who is and who was and who is to come, the Almighty."

> You must also give mental and physical fitness priority.
>
> ~ Jim Otto

REism

It is amazing how the trail of REal Excellence always includes making the goal a priority.

PHYSICAL ACTIVITY

RE

REAL EXCELLENCE

AUGUST 8

Don't Judge A Book By The Cover

Ephesians 1:16-19 ESV – I do not cease to give thanks for you, remembering you in my prayers, that the God of our Lord Jesus Christ, the Father of glory, may give you a spirit of wisdom and of revelation in the knowledge of him, having the eyes of your hearts enlightened, that you may know what is the hope to which he has called you, what are the riches of his glorious inheritance in the saints, and what is the immeasurable greatness of his power toward us who believe, according to the working of his great might

> Open your mind to the world and the many different ways that can be found in it, before making hasty judgments of others. After all, the very same thing that you judge from where you are— may very well be something totally different in meaning on the other side of the world.
>
> ~ C. JoyBell C.

REism

Open your heart to receive Jesus, and God will open your eyes to receive wonderful revelations, wisdom and knowledge of great things.

———— OPEN-MINDEDNESS ————

AUGUST 9

The Gestation Of God's Word

Isaiah 55:1-2 ESV – Come, everyone who thirsts, come to the waters; and he who has no money, come, buy and eat! Come, buy wine and milk without money and without price. Why do you spend your money for that which is not bread, and your labor for that which does not satisfy? Listen diligently to me, and eat what is good, and delight yourselves in rich food.

> Be careful what you feed your body and consider what you feed your senses. Both provide you sustenance that makes you who you are.
>
> ~ Simon Boylan

REism

We cannot live on nutritional food alone. The gestation of God's Word must be actively present in our life. Otherwise everything else is a waste.

WELL-BALANCED NUTRITION

RE
REAL EXCELLENCE

AUGUST 10

You Become What You Think

Proverbs 6:17 ESV – Haughty eyes, a lying tongue, and hands that shed innocent blood,

> We plant seeds that will flower as results in our lives, so best to remove the weeds of anger, avarice, envy and doubt, that peace and abundance may manifest for all.
>
> ~ Dorothy Day

REism

As a man thinks, he becomes. What consumes your thoughts? Remember that you have the power to REdirect your thoughts at any moment.

EXPRESSION OF POSITIVE ATTITUDE

AUGUST 11

Sharing Your Light

John 1:6-8 ESV – There was a man sent from God, whose name was John. He came as a witness, to bear witness about the light, that all might believe through him. He was not the light, but came to bear witness about the light.

> The best way to find yourself is to lose yourself in the service of others.
>
> ~ Mahatma Gandhi

REism

When we share our light with others, we all shine.

How will you share your light today?

AUGUST 12

Joy Comes From Within

Colossians 3:15 ESV – And let the peace of Christ rule in your hearts, to which indeed you were called in one body. And be thankful.

> When you do things from your soul, you feel a river moving in you, a joy.
>
> ~ Rumi

REism

Joy is not determined by the circumstances around it. Joy is the fruit from God that allows happiness to reside within it.

RE
REAL EXCELLENCE

AUGUST 13

Have You Taken The First Step?

John 3:16 ESV – For God so loved the world, that he gave his only Son, that whoever believes in him should not perish but have eternal life.

> People begin to become successful the minute they decide to be.
>
> ~ Harvey Mackay

REism

Have you committed your life to Christ?

If so, praise the Lord for making a life altering decision to become one of God's children.

If not, there is no time like the present to join God's Kingdom.

DEDICATION

RE
REAL EXCELLENCE

AUGUST 14

You Get Out What You Put In

Proverbs 13:4 ESV – The soul of the sluggard craves and gets nothing, while the soul of the diligent is richly supplied.

> The advancement and diffusion of knowledge is the only guardian of true liberty.
>
> ~ James Madison

REism

It has been said that good things come to those who work hard. God says, "He is a rewarder of them that diligently seek Him."

How much do you want?

RE
REAL EXCELLENCE

AUGUST 15

We All See Eye to Eye

Proverbs 19:17 ESV – Whoever is generous to the poor lends to the Lord, and he will repay him for his deed.

> Never look down on anybody unless you're helping him up.
>
> ~ Jesse Jackson

REism

No matter how big your house is, how nice your car is, how big your bank account is, our graves will be the same size. We are all equals!

MANNERS

AUGUST 16

Inspiring Others

Acts 20:35 ESV – In all things I have shown you that by working hard in this way we must help the weak and remember the words of the Lord Jesus, how he himself said, 'It is more blessed to give than to receive.

> Exercise is the chief source of improvement in our faculties.
>
> ~ Hugh Blair

REism

Workout partners can be a great motivator for many people. Just like prayer partners and fellowship groups are valuable for Christians. If you are mentally and physically focused with your workouts, it is time you expand your territory and bring others along.

PHYSICAL ACTIVITY

RE
REAL EXCELLENCE

AUGUST 17

For You and Only You

Luke 21:15 ESV – For I will give you a mouth and wisdom, which none of your adversaries will be able to withstand or contradict.

> Sit down before fact with an open mind. Be prepared to give up every preconceived notion. Follow humbly wherever and to whatever abyss Nature leads or you learn nothing.
>
> ~ Hyman G. Rickover

REism

Know this: What God has for you is for you and only you! But you must engage with God daily and be willing to let go and let God.

OPEN-MINDEDNESS

RE
REAL EXCELLENCE

AUGUST 18

Knowing Is Not Enough

John 13:13 ESV – You call me Teacher and Lord, and you are right, for so I am.

I have been impressed with the urgency of doing. Knowing is not enough; we must apply. Being willing is not enough; we must do.

~ Leonardo da Vinci

REism

If you know, act like you know. Stop talking about eating better and start eating better today! Follow Christ Jesus as a faithful disciple each and every day.

WELL-BALANCED NUTRITION

RE
REAL EXCELLENCE

AUGUST 19

RElease and REplace

Romans 12:2 ESV – Do not be conformed to this world, but be transformed by the renewal of your mind, that by testing you may discern what is the will of God, what is good and acceptable and perfect.

> One of the greatest discoveries of our time is that a man can alter the state of their life by altering the state of their mind.
>
> ~ William James

REism

RElease and REplace preconceived thoughts with the word of God and your mind will be REnewed and REstored.

EXPRESSION OF POSITIVE ATTITUDE

AUGUST 20

Soul to Soul

Proverbs 27:10 – Do not forsake your friend and your father's friend, and do not go to your brother's house in the day of your calamity. Better is a neighbor who is near than a brother who is far away.

> What is a friend? A single soul dwelling in two bodies.
>
> ~ Aristotle

REism

A true friend can feel your highest highs and your lowest lows, and be there to REjoice or comfort you, whichever is needed. Who is your best friend(s)?

RE

REAL EXCELLENCE

AUGUST 21

You Can't Give What Is Not In You

Song of Solomon 4:7 ESV – You are altogether beautiful, my love; there is no flaw in you.

> Know the wholeness, perfection and beauty that you are. Learn to rest in that place within you that is your true home. Find the love you seek, by first finding the love within yourself.
>
> ~ Ravi Shankar

REism

Loving yourself is the first step needed to love others, because you can't give what is not in you.

ENRICHMENT OF SPIRIT

RE
REAL EXCELLENCE

AUGUST 22

Patiently Waiting

Psalm 27:13-14 ESV – I believe that I shall look upon the goodness of the Lord in the land of the living! Wait for the Lord; be strong, and let your heart take courage; wait for the Lord!

> He that can have patience can have what he will.
>
> ~ Benjamin Franklin

REism

If you are not willing to wait, don't complain about the outcome. God answers when He is ready, not when you believe He should answer.

Affirmation: I will patiently wait on God to answer all my prayers and the desires of my heart.

DEDICATION

245

RE
REAL EXCELLENCE

AUGUST 23

A Wider Path

Psalm 119:45 ESV – and I shall walk in a wide place, for I have sought your precepts.

Education breeds confidence. Confidence breeds hope. Hope breeds peace.

~ Confucius

REism

The straight and narrow path can seem even wider when you are walking in the will of God and are armed with the knowledge of His teachings.

EDUCATION

AUGUST 24

The Perfect Day

Galatians 6:10 ESV – So then, as we have opportunity, let us do good to everyone, and especially to those who are of the household of faith.

> You can't live a perfect day without doing something for someone who will never be able to repay you.
>
> ~ John Wooden

REism

God woke you up today, so today is perfect for God. Thank Him! Now go do something for someone else and make your day perfect.

MANNERS

RE

REAL EXCELLENCE

AUGUST 25

More Grip and Less Lip

Proverbs 14:23 ESV – In all toil there is profit, but mere talk tends only to poverty.

> Lack of activity destroys the good condition of every human being, while movement and methodical physical exercise save it and preserve it.
>
> ~ Plato

REism

Action is directly related to productivity. But talking and doing are two totally different things. Talk is just talk! Let's have more Grip and less lip!

RE

REAL EXCELLENCE

AUGUST 26

What Are You Really Saying?

Ecclesiastes 8:1 ESV – Who is like the wise? And who knows the interpretation of a thing? A man's wisdom makes his face shine, and the hardness of his face is changed.

Proper posture sends a positive message since 90% of all communication occurs through body language and how you carry yourself.

~ Cindy Ann Peterson

REism

A person's facial expressions and body language speak volumes to their inner being. Choose to REjoice, because you know God made today and allowed you to be in it.

OPEN-MINDEDNESS

RE
REAL EXCELLENCE

AUGUST 27

Milk Does The Body Good...Pass It On!

1 Peter 2:2-3 ESV – Like newborn infants, long for the pure spiritual milk, that by it you may grow up into salvation—if indeed you have tasted that the Lord is good.

A child's body needs nutrition, not just food.

~ Julie Webb Kelley

REism

Let your desire for God's Word be that of a newborn's desire for milk. We all know that milk does the body good! Pass it on!

WELL-BALANCED NUTRITION

AUGUST 28

All-Powerful

Revelation 4:11 ESV – Worthy are you, our Lord and God, to receive glory and honor and power, for you created all things, and by your will they existed and were created.

> Our ultimate freedom is the right and power to decide how anybody or anything outside ourselves will affect us.
>
> ~ Stephen Covey

REism

Free will is powerful, but the will of God is all-powerful.

EXPRESSION OF POSITIVE ATTITUDE

RE

REAL EXCELLENCE

AUGUST 29

I Can See Clearly Now

Job 42:5-6 ESV – I had heard of you by the hearing of the ear, but now my eye sees you; therefore I despise myself, and repent in dust and ashes.

> The eye through which I see God is the same eye through which God sees me; my eye and God's eye are one eye, one seeing, one knowing, one love.
>
> ~ Meister Eckhart

REism

I once was blind, but now I can see. A REpented heart and REstored RElationship with God is absolutely beautiful!

RELATIONSHIPS

RE
REAL EXCELLENCE

AUGUST 30

Spiritual Fire Burning Inside

Romans 8:28 ESV – And we know that for those who love God all things work together for good, for those who are called according to his purpose.

Love in its essence is spiritual fire.

~ Lucius Annaeus SenecaREism

REism

REal love burns inside us like a spiritual fire, and that fire releases a light to the world that can light up the universe. Let your light shine, so that the love that is in your heart will provide light even through darkness.

ENRICHMENT OF SPIRIT

RE
REAL EXCELLENCE

AUGUST 31

Are You Searching For The City of Eternity?

Hebrews 13:14 ESV – For here we have no lasting city, but we seek the city that is to come.

> There's a way to do it better—find it.
>
> ~ Thomas Edison

REism

The road that leads to the city of Eternity has to go through Christ. So dedicate your life to Christ, and the great city of Eternity will be yours forever.

DEDICATION

SEPTEMBER

RE
REAL EXCELLENCE

SEPTEMBER 1

Faithful to Our Learning

Hebrews 3:6 ESV – but Christ is faithful over God's house as a son. And we are his house if indeed we hold fast our confidence and our boasting in our hope.

> Learning is an ornament in prosperity, a refuge in adversity, and a provision in old age.
>
> ~ Aristotle

REism

Being faithful to our learnings of God's Word will provide guidance while on Earth and will prepare our eternal home as well.

RE
REAL EXCELLENCE

SEPTEMBER 2

The Apple Doesn't Fall Far From The Tree

1 John 3:18 ESV – Little children, let us not love in word or talk but in deed and in truth.

> I seek constantly to improve my manners and graces, for they are the sugar to which all are attracted.
>
> ~ Og Mandino

REism

Good manners and respect start at home. That is why the best soup is made at home!

Set a Godly example, and the children will follow.

MANNERS

RE

SEPTEMBER 3

Commitment

Philippians 2:14-15 ESV – Do all things without grumbling or questioning, that you may be blameless and innocent, children of God without blemish in the midst of a crooked and twisted generation, among whom you shine as lights in the world,

---

There are really only two requirements when it comes to exercise. One is that you do it. The other is that you continue to do it.

~ *The New Glucose Revolution for Diabetes* by Jennie Brand-Miller, Kaye Foster-Powell, Stephen Colagiuri, Alan W. Barclay

---

REism

Motivation is famous for getting people started. But REal commitment is the ability to carry out and continue, long after the mood that made the commitment has passed.

Are you committed?

PHYSICAL ACTIVITY

RE
REAL EXCELLENCE

SEPTEMBER 4

Windshield Washer Fluid

Philippians 1:9 ESV – And it is my prayer that your love may abound more and more, with knowledge and all discernment,

---

Your assumptions are your windows on the world. Scrub them off every once in a while, or the light won't come in.

~ Isaac Asimov

REism

The world can make your windows dirty from time to time, but living in the power of God's Word is the perfect windshield washer fluid needed to clean off the worldly dirt.

Affirmation: I will obey God's Word and use the windshield washer fluid when needed.

OPEN-MINDEDNESS

RE

REAL EXCELLENCE

SEPTEMBER 5

Are You Willing To Work?

Genesis 2:15 ESV – The Lord God took the man and put him in the garden of Eden to work it and keep it.

> There is no drug that can do for you what eating well, moving your body, self-love and mindfulness can.
>
> ~ Bridget Jane

REism

Proper diet, consistent exercise, high self-esteem and mental awareness are all factors that lead to a heathy lifestyle. To live a heathy lifestyle, you must work at it!

SEPTEMBER 6

What I Have is Faith

Luke 10:1-5 ESV – After this the Lord appointed seventy-two others and sent them on ahead of him, two by two, into every town and place where he himself was about to go. And he said to them, "The harvest is plentiful, but the laborers are few. Therefore pray earnestly to the Lord of the harvest to send out laborers into his harvest. Go your way; behold, I am sending you out as lambs in the midst of wolves. Carry no moneybag, no knapsack, no sandals, and greet no one on the road. Whatever house you enter, first say, 'Peace be to this house!'

> Don't let what you cannot do interfere with what you can do.
>
> ~ John Wooden

REism

Walk by faith, and not by sight, because God can see what you can't see. No money, no knapsack, no sandals? No problem! I have faith in my provider God!

EXPRESSION OF POSITIVE ATTITUDE

RE

REAL EXCELLENCE

SEPTEMBER 7

Effective Leadership

Matthew 24:5 ESV – For many will come in my name, saying, "I am the Christ," and they will lead many astray – For many will come in my name, saying, "I am the Christ," and they will lead many astray.

> Our true destiny...is a world built from the bottom up by competent citizens living in solid communities, engaged in and by their places.
>
> ~ David W. Orr

REism

In order to be an effective leader, you must be led by one. There is no better leader than Jesus Christ. Allow Christ to build you into an effective leader that will glorify Him.

RE
REAL EXCELLENCE

SEPTEMBER 8

A Life Well Spent

Psalm 107:1 ESV – Oh give thanks to the Lord, for he is good, for his steadfast love endures forever!

> I have found that if you love life, life will love you back.
>
> ~ Arthur Rubinstein

REism

Be thankful for every breath God gives us. We are alive for God's purpose and His plan. A life spent loving God is a life well spent, because God is love.

RE

REAL EXCELLENCE

SEPTEMBER 9

Talent Alone Won't Cut It

Hebrews 11:6 ESV – And without faith it is impossible to please him, for whoever would draw near to God must believe that he exists and that he rewards those who seek him.

> There is not great talent without great will power.
>
> ~ Honore de Balzac

REism

Faith and Will Power are two characteristics found in all successful people.

RE

REAL EXCELLENCE

SEPTEMBER 10

Point of No Return

Proverbs 3:2 ESV – for length of days and years of life and peace they will add to you.

The mind once enlightened cannot again become dark.

~ Thomas Paine

REism

Your mind has expanded, you are living in the light, and your knowledge is being witnessed for God's glory. Darkness no longer occupies space in your mind.

EDUCATION

RE

REAL EXCELLENCE

SEPTEMBER 11

God is Love

1 Peter 3:9 ESV – Do not repay evil for evil or reviling for reviling, but on the contrary, bless, for to this you were called, that you may obtain a blessing.

The small courtesies sweeten life; the greater ennoble it.

~ Christian Nevell Bovee

REism

Weak people revenge; strong people forgive; Godly people love and are blessed for it!

MANNERS

RE
REAL EXCELLENCE

SEPTEMBER 12

Standing On Your Own Two Feet

1 Thessalonians 4:11-12 ESV – And to aspire to live quietly, and to mind your own affairs, and to work with your hands, as we instructed you, so that you may walk properly before outsiders and be dependent on no one.

> It is your sole responsibility to protect every single one of your days on earth with positive thoughts and beliefs.
>
> ~ Edmond Mbiaka

REism

It is your body, and you must do it! No one can get your body in shape but you.

RE

REAL EXCELLENCE

SEPTEMBER 13

Watch What You See

Matthew 6:23 ESV – But if your eye is bad, your whole body will be full of darkness. If then the light in you is darkness, how great is the darkness.

> When my information changes, I alter my conclusions. What do you do, sir?
>
> ~ John Maynard Keynes

REism

Be mindful of what your eyes take in. It is extremely challenging for the mind to ignore what the eyes see. This is even more important for our children, because the undeveloped mind becomes more curious.

RE

SEPTEMBER 14

Dessertarian

Jeremiah 15:16 ESV – Your words were found, and I ate them, and your words became to me a joy and the delight of my heart, for I am called by your name, O Lord, God of hosts.

I'm not a vegetarian! I'm a dessertarian!

~ Bill Watterson

REism

The Words of God are sweeter than your favorite dessert. Taste it and see how good it is!

RE

SEPTEMBER 15

Bringing Joy and Delight to Others

Philippians 4:1-5 ESV – Therefore, my brothers, whom I love and long for, my joy and crown, stand firm thus in the Lord, my beloved. I entreat Euodia and I entreat Syntyche to agree in the Lord. Yes, I ask you also, true companion, help these women, who have labored side by side with me in the gospel together with Clement and the rest of my fellow workers, whose names are in the book of life. Rejoice in the Lord always; again I will say, Rejoice. Let your reasonableness be known to everyone. The Lord is at hand;

> A positive attitude causes a chain reaction of positive thoughts, events and outcomes. It is a catalyst and it sparks extraordinary results.
>
> ~ Wade Boggs

REism

REjoicing in the Lord is essential in establishing a strong foundation for yourself and others.

Look for opportunities to REjoice in the Lord today!

EXPRESSION OF POSITIVE ATTITUDE

RE
REAL EXCELLENCE

SEPTEMBER 16

Community Relations

Hebrews 3:13 ESV – But exhort one another every day, as long as it is called "today," that none of you may be hardened by the deceitfulness of sin.

> One of the marvelous things about community is that it enables us to welcome and help people in a way we couldn't as individuals.
>
> ~ Jean Vanier

REism

Are you a community leader? Are you engaged in uplifting others through your community work? Starting today look for ways you can better serve your community.

SEPTEMBER 17

A Lifetime Of Thanks

Psalm 50:23 ESV – The one who offers thanksgiving as his sacrifice glorifies me; to one who orders his way rightly I will show the salvation of God!

> Belief is participation. Spirituality is participation. Only when we participate are we in touch with the spiritual.
>
> ~ Anne Wilson Schaef

REism

God's plan involves our fellowship and participation in following His word. It is the doing of God's Word that gives us salvation, and our salvation is worth a lifetime of thanks. Thank God daily!

ENRICHMENT OF SPIRIT

RE
REAL EXCELLENCE

SEPTEMBER 18

Struggling Is Really A Blessing

Revelation 2:10 ESV – Do not fear what you are about to suffer. Behold, the devil is about to throw some of you into prison, that you may be tested, and for ten days you will have tribulation. Be faithful unto death, and I will give you the crown of life.

> The man who goes farthest is generally the one who is willing to do and dare. The sure-thing boat never gets far from shore.
>
> ~ Dale Carnegie

REism

The struggles in our life are one of our greatest blessings. It makes us stronger, sensitive and Godlike. It teaches us that although the world is full of suffering, it is also full of the opportunity to overcome suffering.

RE
REAL EXCELLENCE

SEPTEMBER 19

When You Know Better You Do Better

Romans 8:6 ESV – For to set the mind on the flesh is death, but to set the mind on the Spirit is life and peace.

> There is no wealth like knowledge, no poverty like ignorance.
>
> ~ Ali Bin Abu-Thalib

REism

It is hard to do what you don't know!

SEPTEMBER 20

Nothing in Return

Philippians 2:1-5 ESV – So if there is any encouragement in Christ, any comfort from love, any participation in the Spirit, any affection and sympathy, complete my joy by being of the same mind, having the same love, being in full accord and of one mind. Do nothing from rivalry or conceit, but in humility count others more significant than yourselves. Let each of you look not only to his own interests, but also to the interests of others. Have this mind among yourselves, which is yours in Christ Jesus,

---

We must be as courteous to a man as we are to a picture, which we are willing to give the advantage of a good light.

~ Ralph Waldo Emerson

REism

Help people even when you know they can't help you back.

MANNERS

SEPTEMBER 21

Two Instead Of One

Proverbs 12:24 ESV – The hand of the diligent will rule, while the slothful will be put to forced labor.

> We often miss opportunity because it's dressed in overalls and looks like work.
>
> ~ Thomas A. Edison

REism

Great accomplishments will come to those who work diligently to achieve it. But to work at working less is actually harder, because now you have two jobs instead of one.

Solution: Work hard at whatever you do!

PHYSICAL ACTIVITY

RE
REAL EXCELLENCE

SEPTEMBER 22

Are You a Genius?

Daniel 5:14 ESV – I have heard of you that the spirit of the gods is in you, and that light and understanding and excellent wisdom are found in you.

> Genius has less to do with the size of your mind than how open it is.
>
> ~ Shane Snow

REism

A mind open to living a life committed to God's Word is a genius mind!

RE

SEPTEMBER 23

Getting To The Plus Side Of Good

Psalm 37:4 – Delight yourself in the Lord, and he will give you the desires of your heart.

> Over weeks and months ...you will get addicted to the awesome taste of healthy food...and start wondering why you never did it earlier!
>
> ~ The Fitness Doc

REism

Both good and bad habits are hard to break. So the sooner you get on the plus side of good, the better chance you have of retaining the awesome feelings associated with a heathy lifestyle.

WELL-BALANCED NUTRITION

RE

REAL EXCELLENCE

SEPTEMBER 24

Your Destiny

Galatians 3:28 ESV – There is neither Jew nor Greek, there is neither slave nor free, there is no male and female, for you are all one in Christ Jesus.

> No power in society, no hardship in your condition can depress you, keep you down, in knowledge, power, virtue, influence, but by your own consent.
>
> ~ William Ellery Channing

REism

When you become One in Christ, no one and nothing can interfere with your destiny. You possess the power of God, and He will deliver you to your Godly destiny.

EXPRESSION OF POSITIVE ATTITUDE

RE
REAL EXCELLENCE

SEPTEMBER 25

Quality over Quantity

Colossians 3:1 ESV – If then you have been raised with Christ, seek the things that are above, where Christ is, seated at the right hand of God.

> The quality of your life is the quality of your relationships.
>
> ~ Anthony Robbins

REism

It is the quality of our relationships that matter most, not the quantity.

RE
REAL EXCELLENCE

SEPTEMBER 26

Right On Time

Ephesians 5:20 ESV – Giving thanks always and for everything to God the Father in the name of our Lord Jesus Christ,

---

Even when the future's not certain, our hearts can still be certain — of love and happiness and all that's good.

~ Terri Guillemets

REism

What may be uncertain to us, is known to God. Having faith means being thankful before God has revealed His plan to you. God's timing is always right!

RE

REAL EXCELLENCE

SEPTEMBER 27

Press On, Keep Driving Forward

Luke 9:62 1:17 ESV – Jesus said to him, "No one who puts his hand to the plow and looks back is fit for the kingdom of God."

> Nothing in this world can take the place of persistence. Talent will not; nothing is more common than unsuccessful men with talent. Genius will not; unrewarded genius is almost a proverb. Education will not; the world is full of educated derelicts. Persistence and determination alone are omnipotent. The slogan Press On! has solved and always will solve the problems of the human race.
>
> ~ Calvin Coolidge

REism

If you drive forward looking in the rearview mirror, you will hit something in front of you. It is no coincidence the front windshield of a car is bigger than the rearview mirror. The greatness awaiting you is in front of you. Press On!

DEDICATION

RE

REAL EXCELLENCE

SEPTEMBER 28

God's Will Be Done

2 Chronicles 1:11 ESV – God answered Solomon, "Because this was in your heart, and you have not asked for possessions, wealth, honor, or the life of those who hate you, and have not even asked for long life, but have asked for wisdom and knowledge for yourself that you may govern my people over whom I have made you king,

> ...it's not just learning that's important. It's learning what to do with what you learn and learning why you learn things that matters.
>
> ~ Norton Juster

REism

To expand and grow we must seek God's Word, learn God's Word and ask God for matters of the heart. Ask God what you will, but make sure it lines up with His Will.

God, may Your Will be done. Amen.

EDUCATION

SEPTEMBER 29

The Best Stock Ever

Colossians 3:14 ESV – And above all these put on love, which binds everything together in perfect harmony.

Politeness and consideration for others is like investing pennies and getting dollars back.

~ Thomas Sowell

REism

Kindness is a stock that will never depreciate. Now that is a great investment!

SEPTEMBER 30

You Will Prosper

Proverbs 16:3 ESV – Commit your work to the Lord, and your plans will be established.

It is exercise alone that supports the spirits, and keeps the mind in vigor.

~ Marcus Tullius Cicero

REism

The Christ-driven, mentally stimulated mind and the physically active body shall prosper.

PHYSICAL ACTIVITY

REAL EXCELLENCE

OCTOBER

RE
REAL EXCELLENCE

OCTOBER 1

The Rock

Matthew 7:24 ESV – Everyone then who hears these words of mine and does them will be like a wise man who built his house on the rock.

There is a difference between WISHING for a thing and being READY to receive it. No one is ready for a thing, until he believes he can acquire it. The state of mind must be BELIEF, not mere hope or wish. Open-mindedness is essential for belief.

~ Napoleon Hill

REism

Build your house on the rock of belief in God's Kingdom!

OPEN-MINDEDNESS

OCTOBER 2

A Cupcake Filled With Joy

Luke 24:45 – Then he opened their minds to understand the Scriptures,

> I've never met a problem a proper cupcake couldn't fix.
>
> ~ Sarah Ockler

REism

Don't let hardship and disappointment lead your diet. This will cause you to lean on the wrong ingredients for salvation. Feed your soul spiritual food and enjoy a cupcake filled with joy.

OCTOBER 3

What Are You Seeking?

Psalm 139:23-24 ESV – Search me, O God, and know my heart! Try me and know my thoughts! And see if there be any grievous way in me, and lead me in the way everlasting!.

> Life isn't happening to you; life is responding to you.
>
> ~ Rhonda Byrne

REism

Seek God, and life responds accordingly. Seek self, and life responds accordingly, also.

So seek wisely!

RE
REAL EXCELLENCE

OCTOBER 4

Bringing Others With You

John 10:16 ESV – And I have other sheep that are not of this fold. I must bring them also, and they will listen to my voice. So there will be one flock, one shepherd.

> I alone cannot change the world, but I can cast a stone across the waters to create many ripples.
>
> ~ Mother Teresa

REism

Representing The Lord requires us to stand firm on biblical principles. Let your life be an example to all those who witness your RElationship with Christ.

RELATIONSHIPS

OCTOBER 5

You Are Not Your Mistakes

Proverbs 25:28 ESV – A man without self-control is like a city broken into and left without walls.

If people refuse to look at you in a new light and they can only see you for what you were, only see you for the mistakes you've made, if they don't realize that you are not your mistakes, then they have to go.

~ Steve Maraboli

REism

It is time to grow! In the best and worst of times, always give thanks to God. Every situation is an opportunity to grow closer to God. Don't be misled by who is around you with who is actually with you. God will be with you through the success and failures of life.

Affirmation: I will use my mistakes to grow closer to God.

ENRICHMENT OF SPIRIT

RE

REAL EXCELLENCE

OCTOBER 6

The Best Action Ever Taken

Romans 5:8 ESV – but God shows his love for us in that while we were still sinners, Christ died for us.

> Will is character in action.
>
> ~ William McDougall

REism

God's Willingness to sacrifice His only son is the highest form of dedication and display of character known to man.

RE

OCTOBER 7

Your SAT Test

Philippians 2:3 ESV – Do nothing from selfish ambition or conceit, but in humility count others more significant than yourselves.

> Share your knowledge. It's a way to achieve immortality.
>
> ~ Dalai Lama

REism

Are your motives **S**elfless?

Do your actions show that you **A**spire to please God?

Do you view your sharing of God's Word as a **T**imeless act of kindness?

EDUCATION

RE

REAL EXCELLENCE

OCTOBER 8

Actions Speak Louder Than Words

John 13:35 ESV – By this all people will know that you are my disciples, if you have love for one another.

> The truest form of love is how you behave toward someone, not how you feel about them.
>
> ~ Steve Hall

REism

Words without actions only reveal your vocabulary. REal Love is about Show and Tell!

MANNERS

RE

REAL EXCELLENCE

OCTOBER 9

First Things First

Colossians 3:24 ESV – Knowing that from the Lord you will receive the inheritance as your reward. You are serving the Lord Christ.

> A lack of exercise robs the body of an essential ingredient.
>
> ~ Karen Sessions

REism

Serving the Lord Jesus and serving your physical body will both yield great REwards for your current life and your eternal life. The work is all before you and must be done first!

PHYSICAL ACTIVITY

RE
REAL EXCELLENCE

OCTOBER 10

All Withstanding

Proverbs 13:14-16 ESV – The teaching of the wise is a fountain of life, that one may turn away from the snares of death. Good sense wins favor, but the way of the treacherous is their ruin. In everything the prudent acts with knowledge, but a fool flaunts his folly.

> It is a narrow mind which cannot look at a subject from various points of view.
>
> ~ George Eliot

REism

Thank God for His teachings because a mind powered by God is equipped with the ability to adapt and withstand any and all situations.

OPEN-MINDEDNESS

OCTOBER 11

Buffets Can Be Dangerous

Isaiah 25:6 ESV – On this mountain the Lord of hosts will make for all peoples a feast of rich food, a feast of well-aged wine, of rich food full of marrow, of aged wine well refined.

> I lurched away from the table after a few hours feeling like Elvis in Vegas - fat, drugged, and completely out of it
>
> ~ Anthony Bourdain

REism

The undisciplined eater should stay away from buffet-style meals.

WELL-BALANCED NUTRITION

OCTOBER 12

God Knows You,
Even If You Don't Know Yourself

Psalm 139:1-5 ESV – O Lord, you have searched me and known me! You know when I sit down and when I rise up; you discern my thoughts from afar. You search out my path and my lying down and are acquainted with all my ways. Even before a word is on my tongue, behold, O Lord, you know it altogether. You hem me in, behind and before, and lay your hand upon me.

> Could we change our attitude, we should not only see life differently, but life itself would come to be different.
>
> ~ Katherine Mansfiel

REism

RElinqush your ways and be REcreated in righteousness. Trust the creator of all because God knows all.

——— EXPRESSION OF POSITIVE ATTITUDE ———

OCTOBER 13

Closed Doors

Deuteronomy 31:6 ESV – Be strong and courageous. Do not fear or be in dread of them, for it is the Lord your God who goes with you. He will not leave you or forsake you.

> We have all known the long loneliness and we have learned that the only solution is love and that love comes with community.
>
> ~ Dorothy Day

REism

Don't be discouraged by closed doors. God closes doors that are not for you. So count your blessings and allow God to lead you to your open doors.

RELATIONSHIPS

RE

REAL EXCELLENCE

OCTOBER 14

Treasures Will Fade

Matthew 6:21 ESV – For where your treasure is, there your heart will be also.

> Your sacred space is where you can find yourself over and over again.
>
> ~ Joseph Campbell

REism

Let go of your earthly idols and hold steadfast that all of our blessings come from God. Earthly treasures diminish and fade, but your salvation is forever.

RE
REAL EXCELLENCE

OCTOBER 15

Soul Power

Hebrews 12:1 ESV – Therefore, since we are surrounded by so great a cloud of witnesses, let us also lay aside every weight, and sin which clings so closely, and let us run with endurance the race that is set before us,

> There is no chance, no destiny, no fate, that can hinder or control the firm resolve of a determined soul.
>
> ~ Ella Wheeler Wilcox

REism

Your destiny is located at the end of your soul.

How determined is your soul?

DEDICATION

RE

· REAL EXCELLENCE

OCTOBER 16

You Have The Power, Now Use It!

Hebrews 13:16 ESV – Do not neglect to do good and to share what you have, for such sacrifices are pleasing to God.

Knowledge is Power.

~ Sir Francis Bacon

REism

Studying God's Word will enhance your spiritual growth and give you amazing power to share His words with others.

EDUCATION

OCTOBER 17

Be The Bridge To Someone's Excellence

1 Peter 4:8 ESV – Above all, keep loving one another earnestly, since love covers a multitude of sins.

When you can be the sunshine in someone's life, or the warm rain, why would you be the cold north wind?

~ Robert Brault

REism

REal Excellence is achieved when you help others reach their potential.

MANNERS

OCTOBER 18

REputation

Ephesians 6:7 ESV – Rendering service with a good will as to the Lord and not to man,

---

Exercise is good for your mind, body, and soul.

~ Susie Michelle Cortright

REism

Exercise is great for your mind, body and soul. It can improve your physical appearance, boost your confidence and render a REputation of strength to others. But if you are trying to build your REputation with people, it is time to give up all your human efforts and trust God. Work not in vain to please man, but to please God.

PHYSICAL ACTIVITY

RE

REAL EXCELLENCE

OCTOBER 19

All Day and Every Day

Colossians 1:26-28 ESV – The mystery hidden for ages and generations but now revealed to his saints. To them God chose to make known how great among the Gentiles are the riches of the glory of this mystery, which is Christ in you, the hope of glory. Him we proclaim, warning everyone and teaching everyone with all wisdom, that we may present everyone mature in Christ.

> A truly great book should be read in youth, again in maturity and once more in old age, as a fine building should be seen by morning light, at noon and by moonlight.
>
> ~ Robertson Davies

REism

I will boast all day and every day of the Lord's teachings from the good book. I will not be ashamed to tell His goodness.

OPEN-MINDEDNESS

OCTOBER 20

'Seefood' Diet:
Are Your Eyes Bigger Than Your Stomach?

Matthew 6:22 – The eye is the lamp of the body. So, if your eye is healthy, your whole body will be full of light,

He looks at you like you're crème brûlée.

~ Kelly Moran

REism

Stay far away from the 'Seefood' Diet! Your body will not approve. Educating your mind will train your eye to make healthier food choices.

RE
REAL EXCELLENCE

OCTOBER 21

Small Pleasures

Hebrews 7:25 ESV – Consequently, he is able to save to the uttermost those who draw near to God through him, since he always lives to make intercession for them.

Think big thoughts but relish small pleasures.

~ H. Jackson Brown, Jr.

REism

Dreaming big is great, but make sure your dreams are in alignment to glorify God. Don't be surprised if your big dream is delayed and replaced with small accomplishments along the way. Your small pleasures are used to test your stewardship, so relish in those as well.

EXPRESSION OF POSITIVE ATTITUDE

OCTOBER 22

We Are Family

John 19:26-27 ESV – When Jesus saw his mother and the disciple whom he loved standing nearby, he said to his mother, "Woman, behold, your son!" Then he said to the disciple, "Behold, your mother!" And from that hour the disciple took her to his own home.

> With all things and in all things, we are relatives.
>
> ~Native American (Sioux) Proverb

REism

We are all God's children united in the house of the Lord.

OCTOBER 23

A Grateful Spirit Is Gratifying

Acts 24:3 ESV – In every way and everywhere we accept this with all gratitude.

Cultivate the habit of being grateful for every good thing that comes to you, and to give thanks continuously. And because all things have contributed to your advancement, you should include all things in your gratitude.

~ Ralph Waldo Emerson

REism

Have faith in God's plan for your life. Be grateful for God's blessings each and every day.

OCTOBER 24

It Will Work!

2 Chronicles 7:8-10 ESV – At that time Solomon held the feast for seven days, and all Israel with him, a very great assembly, from Lebo-hamath to the Brook of Egypt. And on the eighth day they held a solemn assembly, for they had kept the dedication of the altar seven days and the feast seven days. On the twenty-third day of the seventh month he sent the people away to their homes, joyful and glad of heart for the prosperity that the Lord had granted to David and to Solomon and to Israel his people.

> If you believe in yourself and have dedication and pride - and never quit, you'll be a winner. The price of victory is high but so are the rewards.
>
> ~ Paul Bryant

REism

You are blessed and covered by the Father. A Godly grace and favor is awaiting you. Stop thinking about all the reasons it won't work and believe the one reason it will work. It will work because God put it on your heart!

Is God calling you to do something?

DEDICATION

RE
REAL EXCELLENCE

OCTOBER 25

Who and What Should You Invest In?

Proverbs 24:5 ESV – A wise man is full of strength, and a man of knowledge enhances his might,

---

> An investment in knowledge always pays the best interest.
>
> ~ Benjamin Franklin

REism

Invest in the person you spend the most time with - YOU! A better you can help you better others.

RE

REAL EXCELLENCE

OCTOBER 26

Life's Defining Moments

1 John 3:17 ESV – But if anyone has the world's goods and sees his brother in need, yet closes his heart against him, how does God's love abide in him?

> Life is short, but there is always time enough for courtesy.
>
> ~ Ralph Waldo Emerson

REism

Two things define you: Your patience when you have nothing, and your attitude when you have everything.

RE
REAL EXCELLENCE

OCTOBER 27

The Best You

1 Timothy 5:8 ESV – But if anyone does not provide for his relatives, and especially for members of his household, he has denied the faith and is worse than an unbeliever.

It is remarkable how one's wits are sharpened by physical exercise.

~author

REism

Is your family getting the best you? Are you sharp and on your game?

As a believer in Christ you have a responsibility first to your family, then relatives. This should be your primary ministry. This responsibility is best served by the best you!

PHYSICAL ACTIVITY

OCTOBER 28

The War Room

Ephesians 6:18-20 ESV – Praying at all times in the Spirit, with all prayer and supplication. To that end keep alert with all perseverance, making supplication for all the saints, and also for me, that words may be given to me in opening my mouth boldly to proclaim the mystery of the gospel, for which I am an ambassador in chains, that I may declare it boldly, as I ought to speak.

> Closed in a room, my imagination becomes the universe, and the rest of the world is missing out.
>
> ~ Criss Jami

REism

There is power in quiet time with God. Quiet time with God brings your heart and soul closer to God's Kingdom.

Do you have a war room? If not, get one!

OPEN-MINDEDNESS

315

RE
REAL EXCELLENCE

OCTOBER 29

A Byproduct Of Poor Decision Making

Romans 8:18 ESV – For I consider that the sufferings of this present time are not worth comparing with the glory that is to be revealed to us.

> Our state of wellness determines our response to any situation. Never allow the busyness of life to distract you from taking care of your well being
>
> ~ Lailah Gifty Akita

REism

Never allow yourself to be so busy that your diet suffers, or you don't partake in God's spiritual food. That is the formula for disaster!

WELL-BALANCED NUTRITION

RE
REAL EXCELLENCE

OCTOBER 30

A Protected Castle

2 Timothy 1:7 ESV – for God gave us a spirit not of fear but of power and love and self-control.

Your positivity can become a castle around you which will protect you from the arrow of negativity.

~ Gurudev Shree Chitrabhanu

REism

Remain positive in all circumstances, and God will protect you from negativity. Keeping a Godly prospective will always be pleasing to our Heavenly Father.

EXPRESSION OF POSITIVE ATTITUDE

OCTOBER 31

Falling Short

Isaiah 1:1-5 ESV – The vision of Isaiah the son of Amoz, which he saw concerning Judah and Jerusalem in the days of Uzziah, Jotham, Ahaz, and Hezekiah, kings of Judah. Hear, O heavens, and give ear, O earth; for the Lord has spoken: "Children have I reared and brought up, but they have rebelled against me. The ox knows its owner, and the donkey its master's crib, but Israel does not know, my people do not understand." Ah, sinful nation, a people laden with iniquity, offspring of evildoers, children who deal corruptly! They have forsaken the Lord, they have despised the Holy One of Israel, they are utterly estranged. Why will you still be struck down? Why will you continue to rebel? The whole head is sick, and the whole heart faint.

I raise up my voice—not so I can shout but so that those without a voice can be heard...we cannot succeed when half of us are held back.

~ Malala Yousafzai

REism

When one falls short of God's glory, we all fall short of His glory. Yes, we are our brother's and sister's keeper. Reach out to a fallen brother or sister today and help bring them back into God's Kingdom.

———————— RELATIONSHIPS ————————

NOVEMBER

RE
REAL EXCELLENCE

NOVEMBER 1

Ignore The Noise

1 Corinthians 15:10 ESV – But by the grace of God I am what I am, and his grace toward me was not in vain. On the contrary, I worked harder than any of them, though it was not I, but the grace of God that is with me.

> The music of hope is everywhere, but to hear it, you need to ignore the muddy jangle of life's hassles.
>
> ~ Christine M. Knight

REism

Here is what you tell the noisemakers: "I can't wait until this storm is over, because I want to tell everyone how God challenged me, how I was able to overcome my challenges, and how I'm a better person for it." Be blinded by the mission God has for you and your life. God's grace and mercy will hold you over until you arrive at your destination.

ENRICHMENT OF SPIRIT

RE

REAL EXCELLENCE

NOVEMBER 2

Where Dreams and Reality Differ

1 Chronicles 26:27 ESV – From spoil won in battles they dedicated gifts for the maintenance of the house of the Lord.

> We all have dreams. But in order to make dreams come into reality, it takes an awful lot of determination, dedication, self-discipline, and effort.
>
> ~ Jesse Owens

REism

Most successful people do not necessarily have the best of everything, they just make the most of everything that comes their way.

NOVEMBER 3

Don't Be Surprised

Luke 12:34 ESV – For where your treasure is, there will your heart be also.

> Learning is a treasure which accompanies its owner everywhere.
>
> ~ Chinese Proverb

REism

Don't be surprised by what you have. You have what you care about because that is what you taught your heart to desire.

NOVEMBER 4

You Can't Buy Class

Ephesians 4:29 ESV – Let no corrupting talk come out of your mouths, but only such as is good for building up, as fits the occasion, that it may give grace to those who hear.

> A man's own manner and character is what most becomes.
>
> ~ Marcus Tulius Cicero

REism

No matter how educated, talented or rich you believe you are, how you treat people ultimately will reveal who you really are.

MANNERS

RE
REAL EXCELLENCE

NOVEMBER 5

Anytime, Anyplace

Ecclesiastes 9:10 ESV – Whatever your hand finds to do, do it with your might, for there is no work or thought or knowledge or wisdom in Sheol, to which you are going.

> Wholesome exercise in the free air, under the wide sky, is the best medicine for body and spirit.
>
> ~ Sarah Louise Arnold

REism

Are time and place holding you hostage from your prayers and physical activity?

Stop searching for the perfect time and place! Do what you can, while you can and wherever you can. You must work while you have physical life.

───────── **PHYSICAL ACTIVITY** ─────────

RE
REAL EXCELLENCE

NOVEMBER 6

I Surrender

Proverbs 3:5 ESV – Trust in the Lord with all your heart, and do not lean on your own understanding.

> We often need to lose sight of our priorities in order to see them.
>
> ~ John Irving

REism

I will go wherever He asks me to go. I will say whatever He would have me say. I will do whatever He asks me to do. I must decrease, so that Christ can increase in me. I'm all in for Christ!

RE
REAL EXCELLENCE

NOVEMBER 7

Hot or Cold—Which Are You?

Revelation 3:16 – So, because you are lukewarm, and neither hot nor cold, I will spit you out of my mouth.

The healthy life: It's not just about losing the weight; it's about losing the lifestyle and mindset that got you there.

~ Steve Maraboli

REism

God doesn't do lukewarm. He is the master of both hot and cold. God loves a heart that burns for Him, and He is readily available to rescue the cold-hearted. But lukewarm is undefined, and therefore rejected by the body. Make a firm commitment to be hot for God, and He will drink away all your unwanted lifestyles.

WELL-BALANCED NUTRITION

RE

REAL EXCELLENCE

NOVEMBER 8

A Farmer's Approach

Proverbs 3:16 ESV – Long life is in her right hand; in her left hand are riches and honor.

> Promise Yourself...To be so strong that nothing can disturb your peace of mind...To talk health, happiness, and prosperity to every person you meet...To make all your friends feel that there is something in them...To look at the sunny side of everything and make your optimism come true.
>
> ~ Christian D. Larson

REism

Planting seeds of joy, happiness, and prosperity are the longevity to a life full of riches and honor.

EXPRESSION OF POSITIVE ATTITUDE

327

NOVEMBER 9

Stewardship

1 Peter 4:10 ESV – As each has received a gift, use it to serve one another, as good stewards of God's varied grace.

Strange is our situation here upon earth. Each of us comes for a short visit, not knowing why, yet sometimes seeming to divine a purpose. From the standpoint of daily life, however, there is one thing we do know: that man is here for the sake of other men.

~ Albert Einstein

REism

Our purpose is to bring glory to God. How are you purposefully living to glorify God and encouraging others to do the same?

RELATIONSHIPS

RE
REAL EXCELLENCE

NOVEMBER 10

The World Of Unlimited Possibilities

Romans 15:13 ESV – May the God of hope fill you with all joy and peace in believing, so that by the power of the Holy Spirit you may abound in hope.

> Once you choose hope, anything's possible.
>
> ~ Christopher Reeve

REism

I will choose hope today and have faith in God's plan for me. Welcome to the world of unlimited possibilities.

NOVEMBER 11

I Give My Heart To You

Deuteronomy 6:4-8 ESV – Hear, O Israel: The Lord our God, the Lord is one. You shall love the Lord your God with all your heart and with all your soul and with all your might. And these words that I command you today shall be on your heart. You shall teach them diligently to your children, and shall talk of them when you sit in your house, and when you walk by the way, and when you lie down, and when you rise. You shall bind them as a sign on your hand, and they shall be as frontlets between your eyes.

> Decide what you want, decide what you are willing to exchange for it. Establish your priorities and go to work.
>
> ~ Haroldson Lafayette Hunt, Jr.

REism

God wants our heart! Trust Him. It is the best exchange you will ever make.

DEDICATION

RE
REAL EXCELLENCE

NOVEMBER 12

Be a Difference Maker

Matthew 5:15 ESV – Nor do people light a lamp and put it under a basket, but on a stand, and it gives light to all in the house.

Knowledge is like money: to be of value it must circulate, and in circulating it can increase in quantity and, hopefully, in value.

~ Louis L'Amour

REism

Educating yourself will change you, but sharing your education will change the world.

NOVEMBER 13

Timeless Return

2 Thessalonians 3:13 ESV – As for you, brothers, do not grow weary in doing good.

> Civility costs nothing and buys everything.
>
> ~ Mary Wortley Montague

REism

Good deeds never grow old and always yield a positive return.

RE

REAL EXCELLENCE

NOVEMBER 14

High Standards

Titus 2:7-8 ESV – Show yourself in all respects to be a model of good works, and in your teaching show integrity, dignity, and sound speech that cannot be condemned, so that an opponent may be put to shame, having nothing evil to say about us.

> Keeping your body healthy is an expression of gratitude to the whole cosmos; the trees, the clouds, everything.
>
> ~ Thich Nhat Hanh

REism

Do all things with REal Excellence in mind so that your work cannot be spoken of evilly or accused of lacking integrity.

PHYSICAL ACTIVITY

RE

REAL EXCELLENCE

NOVEMBER 15

The New You

Romans 12:2 ESV – Do not be conformed to this world, but be transformed by the renewal of your mind, that by testing you may discern what is the will of God, what is good and acceptable and perfect.

> An awake heart is like a sky that pours light.
>
> ~ Hāfez

REism

Don't let the cares of this world define you. Allow the ingested word of God into your heart, change your actions and REnew your mind.

NOVEMBER 16

Sweet Tooth

Genesis 3:19 ESV – By the sweat of your face you shall eat bread, till you return to the ground, for out of it you were taken; for you are dust, and to dust you shall return.

> "Strangely enough, I don't seem to tolerate food in great quantities or when it is too rich anymore."
>
> "That's perfectly all right. Most people dig their graves with their own teeth as it is."
>
> ~ Andrew Ashling, *Bonds of Hate*

REism

Is your sweet tooth digging a grave in your diet?

RE

REAL EXCELLENCE

NOVEMBER 17

Gratitude Affects Your Attitude

Psalm 118:24 ESV – This is the day that the Lord has made; let us rejoice and be glad in it.

> Today is a new beginning, a chance to turn your failures into achievements & your sorrows into so goods. No room for excuses.
>
> ~ Joel Brown

REism

REjoicing is a sign of gratitude to God. Let the REjoicing begin!

RE
REAL EXCELLENCE

NOVEMBER 18

Love At First Sight

Ephesians 4:2 ESV – with all humility and gentleness, with patience, bearing with one another in love,

---

> There is never a time or place for true love. It happens accidentally, in a heartbeat, in a single flashing, throbbing moment.
>
> ~ Sarah Dessen

REism

Does love at first sight really happen? If you believe it does, please email your story to REal Excellence at info@realexcellenceinc.com.

NOVEMBER 19

Seek The Word and Gain Salvation

John 5:39 ESV – You search the Scriptures because you think that in them you have eternal life; and it is they that bear witness about me,

---

> The soul can do without everything except the word of God, without which none at all of its wants are provided for.
>
> ~ Martin Luther

REism

In your quest to seek God, be enlightened by his written and living word, The Bible.

ENRICHMENT OF SPIRIT

NOVEMBER 20

Cloudy Day

Psalm 91:1-16 ESV – He who dwells in the shelter of the Most High will abide in the shadow of the Almighty. I will say to the Lord, "My refuge and my fortress, my God, in whom I trust." For he will deliver you from the snare of the fowler and from the deadly pestilence. He will cover you with his pinions, and under his wings you will find refuge; his faithfulness is a shield and buckler. You will not fear the terror of the night, nor the arrow that flies by day,

> The man who can drive himself further once the effort gets painful is the man who will win.
>
> ~ Roger Bannister

REism

Faith is moving forward even when things don't make sense, trusting that in hindsight everything will become clear.

— DEDICATION —

NOVEMBER 21

Knowledge is Freedom

Galatians 5:1 ESV – For freedom Christ has set us free; stand firm therefore, and do not submit again to a yoke of slavery.

> Education is a better safeguard of liberty than a standing army.
>
> ~ Edward Everett

REism

Are you free?

NOVEMBER 22

Changing Darkness to Light

Romans 15:2 ESV – Let each of us please his neighbor for his good, to build him up.

Today, give a stranger one of your smiles. It might be the only sunshine he sees all day.

~ H. Jackson Brown, Jr.

REism

You never know when your light will turn someone else's dark day around.

MANNERS

RE
REAL EXCELLENCE

NOVEMBER 23

Fruits of Your Labor

2 Timothy 2:6 ESV – It is the hard-working farmer who ought to have the first share of the crops.

> Health and cheerfulness naturally beget each other.
>
> ~ Joseph Addison

REism

You deserve to be the first partaker of your work. Enjoy the fruits of your labor!

PHYSICAL ACTIVITY

RE

REAL EXCELLENCE

NOVEMBER 24

God Is The Best Cardiologist in the World

Jeremiah 9:24 ESV – But let him who boasts boast in this, that he understands and knows me, that I am the Lord who practices steadfast love, justice, and righteousness in the earth. For in these things I delight, declares the Lord.

> Listen to God with a broken heart. He is not only the doctor who mends it, but also the father who wipes away the tears
>
> ~ Criss Jami

REism

Give your heart to God, and He will lead your mind to an amazing place where all your troubles will disappear, and your life's work will be celebrated.

OPEN-MINDEDNESS

343

RE
REAL EXCELLENCE

NOVEMBER 25

Selections and Limitations
Are The Keys to a Healthy Diet

Psalm 141:3 ESV – Set a guard, O Lord, over my mouth; keep watch over the door of my lips!

Eat food. Not too much. Mostly plants.

~ Michael Pollan

REism

It is not just what you eat, it is also how much you eat. Be very mindful of your food selections and overall consumption.

NOVEMBER 26

Wasted Energy

Luke 10:10-13 ESV – But whenever you enter a town and they do not receive you, go into its streets and say, 'Even the dust of your town that clings to our feet we wipe off against you. Nevertheless know this, that the kingdom of God has come near.' I tell you, it will be more bearable on that day for Sodom than for that town. "Woe to you, Chorazin! Woe to you, Bethsaida! For if the mighty works done in you had been done in Tyre and Sidon, they would have repented long ago, sitting in sackcloth and ashes.

To be upset over what you don't have is to waste what you do have.

~ Ken S. Keyes, Jr.

REism

As God's children, we have every resource necessary to succeed. Focus on what you have, because what you have is from God.

How will you share your God-given resources with others?

EXPRESSION OF POSITIVE ATTITUDE

RE

REAL EXCELLENCE

NOVEMBER 27

Preferential Treatment Can Derail Leadership

Matthew 20:28 ESV – even as the Son of Man came not to be served but to serve, and to give his life as a ransom for many.

> In real life, the most practical advice for leaders is not to treat pawns like pawns, nor princes like princes, but all persons like persons.
>
> ~ James MacGregor Burns

REism

True leaders serve, and true servants lead.

How will you lead and serve others today?

RE

REAL EXCELLENCE

NOVEMBER 28

Stop Being A Control Freak

Ephesians 6:16-20 ESV – In all circumstances take up the shield of faith, with which you can extinguish all the flaming darts of the evil one; and take the helmet of salvation, and the sword of the Spirit, which is the word of God, praying at all times in the Spirit, with all prayer and supplication. To that end keep alert with all perseverance, making supplication for all the saints, and also for me, that words may be given to me in opening my mouth boldly to proclaim the mystery of the gospel, for which I am an ambassador in chains, that I may declare it boldly, as I ought to speak.

> I believe that Everything Happens for a Reason. People change, so that you can learn to let go. Things go wrong, so that you can appreciate them when they're right.
>
> ~ Marilyn Monroe

REism

You are not in control! Live, Learn and Let God! It is free, REjuvenating and the REward is an eternal life with God.

ENRICHMENT OF SPIRIT

RE
REAL EXCELLENCE

NOVEMBER 29

True Power

Psalm 23:1-6 ESV – A Psalm of David. The Lord is my shepherd; I shall not want. He makes me lie down in green pastures. He leads me beside still waters. He restores my soul. He leads me in paths of righteousness for his name's sake. Even though I walk through the valley of the shadow of death, I will fear no evil, for you are with me; your rod and your staff, they comfort me. You prepare a table before me in the presence of my enemies; you anoint my head with oil; my cup overflows.

> I learned patience, perseverance, and dedication. Now I really know myself, and I know my voice. It's a voice of pain and victory.
>
> ~ Anthony Hamilton

REism

Knowing others is intelligence; knowing yourself is true wisdom. Mastering others is strength; mastering yourself is true power.

DEDICATION

NOVEMBER 30

Investment Plan

2 Timothy 2:15 ESV – Do your best to present yourself to God as one approved, a worker who has no need to be ashamed, rightly handling the word of truth.

> Education is not an expense, but it is the capital ready to be invested. The return depends on the wisdom you gained.
>
> ~ Debasish Mridha

REism

You are your best investment. How much have you invested in you?

DECEMBER

RE
REAL EXCELLENCE

DECEMBER 1

A Hand Up

Matthew 5:42 ESV – Give to the one who begs from you, and do not refuse the one who would borrow from you.

> Not he who has much is rich, but he who gives much.
>
> ~ Erich Fromm

REism

Give richly, and God will bless you beyond your means!

MANNERS

RE
REAL EXCELLENCE

DECEMBER 2

Workout Praise Song

Galatians 6:9 ESV – And let us not grow weary of doing good, for in due season we will reap, if we do not give up.

> Life is not merely to be alive, but to be well.
>
> ~ Marcus Valerius Martial

REism

Have an attitude of praise unto God while working. He will strengthen you until the end. When you feel weary and tired, have a praise song in your heart, for you will not reap or faint.

What is your praise song?

PHYSICAL ACTIVITY

RE
REAL EXCELLENCE

DECEMBER 3

Traffic Ahead, Proceed With Caution

Proverbs 14:16 ESV – One who is wise is cautious and turns away from evil, but a fool is reckless and careless.

> When you make a choice, you change the future.
>
> ~ Deepak Chopra

REism

A man of God is wise and will not run into traffic with blinders on. It would take a fool to try. It is wise to trust in Jesus to keep you on the right path.

RE
REAL EXCELLENCE

DECEMBER 4

Feeding Those In Need

Matthew 25:35 ESV – For I was hungry and you gave me food, I was thirsty and you gave me drink, I was a stranger and you welcomed me,

---

When we give cheerfully and accept gratefully, everyone is blessed.

~ Maya Angelou

REism

Look for ways to share your blessing with others this Holiday Season. Feeding those in need, or providing the means to a facilitator of those in need, is great stewardship of sharing God's blessings.

WELL-BALANCED NUTRITION

RE

REAL EXCELLENCE

DECEMBER 5

Passing Your Blessings Forward

1 Peter 3:9 ESV – Do not repay evil for evil or reviling for reviling, but on the contrary, bless, for to this you were called, that you may obtain a blessing.

> Every thought is a seed. If you plant crab apples, don't count on harvesting Golden Delicious.
>
> ~ Bill Meyer

REism

Encouragement and love is a seed that should be deposited daily. Recall who deposited seeds of love and encouragement into your life and pay it forward.

EXPRESSION OF POSITIVE ATTITUDE

DECEMBER 6

Questioning Your Truths

Psalm 40:4 ESV – Blessed is the man who makes the Lord his trust, who does not turn to the proud, to those who go astray after a lie!

> Trust men and they will be true to you: treat them greatly and they will show themselves great.
>
> ~ Ralph Waldo Emerson

REism

Trust is the foundation of a lasting relationship that starts with trusting yourself. Telling one lie can bring all your truths into question.

Are you trustworthy in your personal and professional relationships?

RELATIONSHIPS

RE
REAL EXCELLENCE

DECEMBER 7

The Rules Of Goodness

Psalm 23:6 ESV – Surely goodness and mercy shall follow me all the days of my life, and I shall dwell in the house of the Lord forever.

> Give goodness to the day and before you know it, the day will be giving goodness to you.
>
> ~ Terri Guillemets

REism

Five simplest rules to goodness:

1. Free your heart from hatred.
2. Free your mind from worries.
3. Live a simple life.
4. Give more!
5. Expect less!

RE
REAL EXCELLENCE

DECEMBER 8

Soaring Like an Eagle

1 Chronicles 26:26 ESV – This Shelomoth and his brothers were in charge of all the treasuries of the dedicated gifts that David the king and the heads of the fathers' houses and the officers of the thousands and the hundreds and the commanders of the army had dedicated.

> Most of us serve our ideals by fits and starts. The person who makes a success of living is the one who sees his goal steadily and aims for it unswervingly. That is dedication.
>
> ~ Cecil B. DeMille

REism

Celebrate your success and stand when adversity comes, for when the storm clouds come in, the eagles soar, while the small birds take cover. Which one are you: an eagle or a small bird?

DEDICATION

RE

REAL EXCELLENCE

DECEMBER 9

You Reap What You Sow

2 Corinthians 9:6 ESV – The point is this: whoever sows sparingly will also reap sparingly, and whoever sows bountifully will also reap bountifully.

> If you have knowledge, let others light their candles in it.
>
> ~ Margaret Fuller

REism

What are you reaping?

RE
REAL EXCELLENCE

DECEMBER 10

You Are Not The Judge

Romans 11:22 ESV – Note then the kindness and the severity of God: severity toward those who have fallen, but God's kindness to you, provided you continue in his kindness. Otherwise you too will be cut off.

Consideration for others is the basic of a good life, a good society.

~ Confucius

REism

We don't need a finger that points out our mistakes, but instead gentle hands that lead.

Let God do His job!

MANNERS

RE
REAL EXCELLENCE

DECEMBER 11

Directing Your Energy

Proverbs 12:11 ESV – Whoever works his land will have plenty of bread, but he who follows worthless pursuits lacks sense.

> Without health, there is no point. To anything.
>
> ~ Everett Mámor

REism

It is important that you evaluate how you spend your time and energy each day. Be assured that your daily activities are benefitting yourself and others.

PHYSICAL ACTIVITY

RE
REAL EXCELLENCE

DECEMBER 12

The Sky Is The Limit

Proverbs 23:12 ESV – Apply your heart to instruction and your ear to words of knowledge.

The sky is the daily bread of the eyes.

~ Ralph Waldo Emerson

REism

Children of God are obedient to God's Word, and for them the sky is the limit!

Go for it! God is with you.

RE

REAL EXCELLENCE

DECEMBER 13

Starting Your Day Off Right

John 21:12 ESV – Jesus said to them, "Come and have breakfast." Now none of the disciples dared ask him, "Who are you?" They knew it was the Lord.

Breakfast is the most important meal of the day. When you feed yourself what your body needs when it needs it, that's love. So give your bod some TLC and sit down and enjoy a good, substantial breakfast.

~ Kathy Freston

REism

Don't miss breakfast, otherwise your body will have to play catch up all day. Missing breakfast can also lead to overeating later in the day.

WELL-BALANCED NUTRITION

DECEMBER 14

Action!

Romans 12:9-10 ESV – Let love be genuine. Abhor what is evil; hold fast to what is good. Love one another with brotherly affection. Outdo one another in showing honor.

> If you don't like something, change it. If you can't change it. Change your attitude.
>
> ~ Maya Angelou

REism

Love is a verb and a verb is action.

Are you actively showing love to others, or are you just saying the word?

RE
REAL EXCELLENCE

DECEMBER 15

United We Can Conquer All

Philippians 2:2 ESV – complete my joy by being of the same mind, having the same love, being in full accord and of one mind.

> If you want to go quickly, go alone. If you want to go far, go together.
>
> ~ African Proverb

REism

Where there is unity, there is strength. A union is only as strong as its weakest link!

RELATIONSHIPS

RE
REAL EXCELLENCE

DECEMBER 16

The Rebirth

John 11:41 ESV – So they took away the stone. And Jesus lifted up his eyes and said, "Father, I thank you that you have heard me.

> A rebirth out of spiritual adversity causes us to become new creatures.
>
> ~ James E. Faust

REism

God selects the soil in which we grow. Take ownership of the message that God intends for us to learn from Him and apply His teachings to our actions. Living in God's Word and allowing the Holy Spirit to dwell in our soul is a rebirth.

RE
REAL EXCELLENCE

DECEMBER 17

A Lesson About Rain

1 Kings 5:5 ESV – And so I intend to build a house for the name of the Lord my God, as the Lord said to David my father, "Your son, whom I will set on your throne in your place, shall build the house for my name."

There are no secrets to success. It is the result of preparation, hard work, and learning from failure.

~ Colin Powell

REism

Everybody wants happiness; nobody wants pain. But you cannot have a rainbow without a little rain. When God anoints His leaders, He will always provide the strength needed to weather any storm. You will become His living testimony.

--- **DEDICATION** ---

DECEMBER 18

Maturity

1 Corinthians 13:11 ESV – When I was a child, I spoke like a child, I thought like a child, I reasoned like a child. When I became a man, I gave up childish ways.

The greatest enemy of knowledge is not ignorance; it is the illusion of knowledge.

~ Stephen Hawking

REism

Eights words that define maturity—I don't know, but I'm willing to learn!

EDUCATION

DECEMBER 19

The 3 M's of Friendship

1 Peter 3:8 ESV – Finally, all of you, have unity of mind, sympathy, brotherly love, a tender heart, and a humble mind.

Respect for ourselves guides our morals;
respect for others guides our manners.

~ Laurence Sterne

REism

Morals, Manners and Maturity will keep your friendships on solid ground.

MANNERS

RE

REAL EXCELLENCE

DECEMBER 20

Hired and Fed By God

Genesis 2:15 ESV – The Lord God took the man and put him in the garden of Eden to work it and keep it.

> A healthy body is the guest-chamber of the soul; a sick, its prison.
>
> ~ Francis Bacon

REism

Know that it is God that hired us to work and requires us to work, so that we may be able to eat freely and glorify Him with our physical and mental strength.

PHYSICAL ACTIVITY

DECEMBER 21

Solid Foundation

Proverbs 24:3-7 ESV – By wisdom a house is built, and by understanding it is established; by knowledge the rooms are filled with all precious and pleasant riches. A wise man is full of strength, and a man of knowledge enhances his might, for by wise guidance you can wage your war, and in abundance of counselors there is victory.

> Even in an abstract dimension, ideas built on flawed foundations will fail.
>
> ~ Romina Russell

REism

Let Jesus be your wise counselor and the Holy Spirit be your helper. Your mentors will provide guidance, and you will walk in victory on a foundation agreeable to the Lord.

OPEN-MINDEDNESS

DECEMBER 22

The Best Insurance Policy

Ephesians 6:13 ESV – Therefore take up the whole armor of God, that you may be able to withstand in the evil day, and having done all, to stand firm.

> And I believe that the best buy in public health today must be a combination of regular physical exercise and a healthy diet.
>
> ~ Julie Bishop

REism

A well-maintained body can avoid major breakdowns. Specialize in tune-ups and daily maintenance. You are your own earthly health provider! Your Heavenly provider is God, and He has you covered with the whole armor of protection.

WELL-BALANCED NUTRITION

DECEMBER 23

It's Only Temporary

1 Peter 4:1 ESV – Since therefore Christ suffered in the flesh, arm yourselves with the same way of thinking, for whoever has suffered in the flesh has ceased from sin,

---

> Learn to smile at every situation. See it as an opportunity to prove your strength and ability.
>
> ~ Joe Brown

REism

Suffering is temporary, but strength is everlasting. Ask God for strength with all situations.

EXPRESSION OF POSITIVE ATTITUDE

DECEMBER 24

Utopia of Love

1 John 4:18 ESV – There is no fear in love, but perfect love casts out fear. For fear has to do with punishment, and whoever fears has not been perfected in love.

> You've gotta dance like there's nobody watching, Love like you'll never be hurt, Sing like there's nobody listening, And live like it's heaven on earth.
>
> ~ African Proverb

REism

It is organic, you feel free to be you, blind trust is present, all your fears have been cast aside, unconditional support is a two-way street, and life feels perfect! You are experiencing the Utopia of Love!

RELATIONSHIPS

RE

REAL EXCELLENCE

DECEMBER 25

The Perfect Gift

James 1:17 ESV – Every good gift and every perfect gift is from above, coming down from the Father of lights with whom there is no variation or shadow due to change.

> What you are is God's gift to you, what you become is your gift to God.
>
> ~ Hans Urs von Balthasar, *Prayer*

REism

As a believer and follower of Christ I have given God the perfect gift by hearing God's Word, believing God's Word, repenting my sins to God, confessing that Christ is the Savior and being baptized for the remission of my sins. Surrendering my life to God is the perfect gift!

Merry Christmas!

DECEMBER 26

Are You Hallucinating?

Numbers 18:14 ESV – Every devoted thing in Israel shall be yours.

> You need to make a commitment, and once you make it, then life will give you some answers.
>
> ~ Les Brown

REism

Success minus devotion and commitment equals hallucination!

The answers are disguised as work!

RE
REAL EXCELLENCE

DECEMBER 27

The Facts of Life

Psalm 23:1-6 ESV – The Lord is my shepherd; I shall not want. He makes me lie down in green pastures. He leads me beside still waters. He restores my soul. He leads me in paths of righteousness for his name's sake. Even though I walk through the valley of the shadow of death, I will fear no evil, for you are with me; your rod and your staff, they comfort me. You prepare a table before me in the presence of my enemies; you anoint my head with oil; my cup overflows. Surely goodness and mercy shall follow me all the days of my life, and I shall dwell in the house of the Lord forever.

> Before you speak, listen. Before you write, think. Before you spend, earn. Before you invest, investigate. Before you criticize, wait. Before you pray, forgive. Before you quit, try. Before you retire, save. Before you die, give.
>
> ~ William A. Ward

REism

Learning and applying the facts of life will lead you to the gates of Heaven.

EDUCATION

RE

REAL EXCELLENCE

DECEMBER 28

The Power is Yours

Acts 20:35 ESV – In all things I have shown you that by working hard in this way we must help the weak and remember the words of the Lord Jesus, how he himself said, "It is more blessed to give than to receive."

Kindness is in our power, even when fondness is not.

~ Samuel Johnson

REism

Sometimes we don't need keen eyes that always see faults, but open arms that accept. Acts of kindness are pleasing to God.

MANNERS

RE

REAL EXCELLENCE

DECEMBER 29

Let's Do It Again

2 Timothy 4:7 ESV – I have fought the good fight, I have finished the race, I have kept the faith.

> The moment of victory is much too short to live for that and nothing else.
>
> ~ Martina Navratilova

REism

Congratulations on a job well done this year! The only thing better than victory itself is another victory. Win your workout today and keep winning…into the New Year and beyond!

PHYSICAL ACTIVITY

RE

REAL EXCELLENCE

DECEMBER 30

Lost and Found

2 Timothy 2:7 ESV – Think over what I say, for the Lord will give you understanding in everything.

> ...sometimes when you are lost for direction, you are open to a new way of seeing.
>
> ~ Lauren Lola

REism

God has the best navigation system for those who are lost. Open your mind, allow your heart to be changed and bear witness to the impact God will have on your life.

OPEN-MINDEDNESS

DECEMBER 31

Your New BFF

3 John 1:2 ESV – Beloved, I pray that all may go well with you and that you may be in good health, as it goes well with your soul.

A journey with a thousand miles begins with a single step.

~ John Mackey

REism

The best medicine for your body is the food you eat. If you have never done so before, consult with a nutritionist and discuss your food choices. Your nutritionist will become your new Best Friend Forever (BFF)!

CONCLUSION: "THE GOOD LIFE"!

What is "The Good Life"?

Living your life for Christ is "The Good Life"! When you live for Christ it gives you a true authentic relationship with God. This relationship with God can only be fulfilled by:

- Hearing God's Word

- Believing God's Word

- Repenting of your sins

- Confessing that Christ is the Savior

- Being baptized for the remission of your sins

It is New Year's Eve and you have just finished feeding your heart and soul the last message of your spiritual food from the complete year of *REal Life EMPOWERED* daily devotional. You are covered with the full body of God's armor. As many others ponder various New Year's resolutions, you feel completely transformed and eager to continue your walk and growth with Christ. Your commitment throughout the year has yielded a return that has transformed every aspect of your life. How does it feel to be living "The Good Life"?

Now with a more educated mind, enriched heart and EMPOWERED soul from reading *REal Life EMPOWERED* daily devotional, you are REformed, REvived and REjuvenated to do God's Work on Earth. Continue to learn, grow and share the gospel with believers to feed all souls, and help bring the souls of non-believers to Christ. Stay humble, prayed up and give the glory to God. Keep Christ first in your life, and you will always have a life.

Thank God for our blessings, and let's continue to be a blessing to others!

REAL EXCELLENCE

REal Love

For God so loved the world, that he gave his only Son, that whoever believes in him should not perish but have eternal life.

~ John 3:16 ESV

REal Life EMPOWERED

I Am the Way, and the Truth, and the Life

"Let not your hearts be troubled. Believe in God; believe also in me. In my Father's house are many rooms. If it were not so, would I have told you that I go to prepare a place for you? And if I go and prepare a place for you, I will come again and will take you to myself, that where I am you may be also. And you know the way to where I am going." Thomas said to him, "Lord, we do not know where you are going. How can we know the way?" Jesus said to him, "I am the way, and the truth, and the life. No one comes to the Father except through me. If you had known me, you would have known my Father also. From now on you do know him and have seen him."

~ John 14:1-7 ESV

The end of you is the beginning of Him, so in REal Life the end is really the beginning.

RE

REAL EXCELLENCE

ABOUT THE AUTHOR

Bo Porter is living proof that, if given a bridge of opportunity, anyone can reach the peak of his or her potential. He possesses fortitude, a burning desire to attain ambitious goals, and the work ethic it takes to reach and sustain success. An accomplished professional athlete, Major League Baseball (MLB) Executive, entrepreneur, business developer and philanthropist. Bo knows how to empower himself and others to attain the highest levels of personal and professional achievement.

Born and raised in the heart of inner-city Newark, New Jersey, Bo faced many obstacles and long odds of overcoming his environment and the circumstances surrounding his upbringing. His first bridge of opportunity came in the form of a kind gesture from a neighborhood friend. This one gesture opened the first of many doors that would propel Bo though a series of accomplishments that continue to this day.

Bo was drafted by the Cubs in 1993, and earned his Communications degree from the University of Iowa in 1994. He played in the Major Leagues for the Cubs, Oakland A's and Texas Rangers. He also coached for the Miami Marlins, Arizona Diamondbacks, Washington Nationals, and Atlanta Braves.

At the age of 40, the Houston Astros hired Bo as Manager, making him the youngest manager in MLB at the time. He completed the trifecta of the MLB hierarchy when he was named Special Assistant General Manager of the Atlanta Braves. He was later promoted to Director of the Major League Baseball Players Association Players Trust & Player Development. Bo transitioned into broadcast media when he was hired by the Mid-Atlantic Sports Network (MASN) as the Pre & Post Game Analyst for the World Series Champions Washington Nationals. He currently works for the MLB Commissioner's Office as the Director of Coaching Development and is a broadcast analyst for MLB Network.

Bo is a nationally acclaimed Keynote Speaker, known as "The Coach of Champions." He's the Founder and Chairman of the Board for Bo Porter Academy, Founding President of Future All-Stars Sports Development Academy, CEO of Bo Porter Enterprise, Founder and CEO of CORE Multimedia Group and the author of two books REal Life EMPOWERED and The END GAME.

Bo received Mayoral Proclamations and Keys to the City from the Mayors of both Newark, NJ and Houston, Texas. Bo received a Proclamation from Houston's Mayor Sylvester Turner on February 7, 2017, a day that was proclaimed Bo Porter Day in Houston, Texas. Bo also received a Proclamation from the Essex County Executive Joe DiVincenzo on December 13, 2012, a day that was proclaimed Bo Porter Day in Essex County, New Jersey. On May 5, 2015, Newark, New Jersey's Mayor Ras Baraka renamed Green Acres Park the Marquis "Bo" Porter Sports Complex. The mayor said, "The renaming of this park is a tribute to Bo's lifetime accomplishments and commitment to our great city." Bo was inducted into the Newark Athletic Hall of Fame in 2001. He was inducted into the Weequahic High School Alumni Association Hall of Fame in 2018.

Bo is a visionary who creates an environment that centers around positive movements and transformational growth. Bo is an entrepreneur at heart, a change agent for all that is good and a true champion. He lives in Missouri City, Texas with his wife Dr. Heather Brown and their three sons Bryce, Jaxon and Jace.

www.ingramcontent.com/pod-product-compliance
Lightning Source LLC
Chambersburg PA
CBHW070016100426
42740CB00013B/2513